BRIGHT NOTES

THE DIVINE COMEDY BY DANTE

Intelligent Education

INFLUENCE
PUBLISHERS

Nashville, Tennessee

BRIGHT NOTES: The Divine Comedy
www.BrightNotes.com

ISBN: 978-1-645420-74-3 (Paperback)
ISBN: 978-1-645420-75-0 (eBook)

Published in accordance with the U.S. Copyright Office Orphan Works and Mass Digitization report of the register of copyrights, June 2015.

Originally published by Monarch Press.
Jules Gelernt, 1964
2019 Edition published by Influence Publishers.

Interior design by Lapiz Digital Services. Cover Design by Thinkpen Designs.

Printed in the United States of America.

Library of Congress Cataloging-in-Publication Data forthcoming.
Names: Intelligent Education
Title: BRIGHT NOTES: The Divine Comedy
Subject: STU004000 STUDY AIDS / Book Notes

CONTENTS

INTRODUCTION TO DANTE

....

THE DIVINE COMEDY

This is an **epic** poem depicting an imaginary journey through Hell, Purgatory, and Paradise. It is presented in the form of a vision experienced by the author in the year 1300, when, as he puts it, he was at the mid-point of his journey through life. Yet, although the poem stages an imaginary voyage through the realms of the afterlife, it deals with human experience. For one thing, the hero, Dante himself, encounters on his way the souls of people who were once alive and whose experiences as human beings are revealed and evaluated. Furthermore, the poem displays an intense interest in the social and political events of the times. On both counts, then, human events are an important part of Dante's poem. And lastly, Hell, Purgatory, and Paradise were as real to Dante and his contemporaries as the physical world they lived in. Dante's **epic** is, therefore, not a flight into fantasy; it is an imaginative work which, coming to grips with the problems of life, seeks to interpret the meaning of human existence.

THE REALITY OF THE SPIRITUAL WORLD

The world of Spirit - the realms of eternity through which Dante Travels - is not a vague abstraction for Dante, but a concrete reality. And it is one of the glories of his achievement as a poet that he is able to translate his sense of that world's real existence into images which enable us to visualize it. But even such visualization is not an end in itself. The moral, philosophical, and theological truths which Dante uncovers on his imaginary journey apply to human life everywhere and for all time, and his vision is accompanied by the specific mission of bringing the truths he has learned to the awareness of mankind. These truths are to shed light on the meaning of man's life and serve as guides for the conduct of private and public life in this world.

DANTE'S VISION AS PERSONAL EXPERIENCE

The Divine Comedy is therefore more than an ingenious formulation, through images, of philosophic and theological doctrine. Like all great epics, it is a presentation and interpretation of the nature of human existence. But if the poet is to communicate his meaning successfully - if the vision is to come alive for us, he must not only make us see and understand the truth he perceives, he must also make us feel it. In other words, he must make us live through the experience with him. This direct communication of the feel of experience is accomplished by means of the hero, with whom we identify: through our identification, we not only observe the hero's experience, but share in it as well. Dante makes himself the hero of his **epic**. Speaking in the first person, he can interpret his experience for us by commenting on it. And insofar as he is an actor in his drama - insofar as what happens, happens to him - we can put ourselves in his place and experience in some measure what he experiences. Dante's poem is a Christian **epic** which takes as its subject the soul's pilgrimage from sin to salvation. Specifically, it is the progress of Dante's soul toward salvation that is at issue. It is in this way that the poem becomes a meaningful experience for its readers. For Dante's unshakable faith in God's concern with his personal salvation assures us that God is equally interested in each and every human being's salvation. In short, by focusing on his personal experience, Dante gives his poem universal meaning.

THE IMPORTANCE OF LOVE

The underlying **theme** of the Divine Comedy is that love is the force which holds the universe together and links it to God, its Creator. Like a magnet, it draws men's souls to their Maker. It is love, therefore, which is the motivating force behind Dante's spiritual journey. But love is not just an abstract principle to be defined philosophically; it is an intense psychic experience in which a man's desire is focused on a specific object. In Dante's case, it is his passion for Beatrice which starts him on the road to salvation. It is she who forces him to raise his sights ever higher until he is brought face to face with God. At the end of the poem he feels at one with "the Love that moves the sun and the other stars," and, on one level, Dante's progress consists in nothing more than the gradual deepening of his understanding of what was at first a purely emotional experience. Here again, the movement of the poem is from the personal to the universal level, but the personal experience is never lost sight of, and it is this feature of Dante's poem which makes it possible for us to follow him and make his experience our own.

DANTE'S LOVE FOR BEATRICE

The ups and downs of his passion for the incomparable Beatrice had been recorded by Dante in an earlier work, the Vita Nuova ("New" or "Young Life"), and we must consider that relationship briefly if we want to understand her function in the scheme of his salvation. It was the sight of Beatrice's unutterable beauty which first set in motion the long and difficult process of spiritual rebirth and personal salvation which finally culminates in the closing cantos of *Paradiso* (the third and last section of *the Divine Comedy*). For in loving Beatrice, Dante unwittingly loved the beauty of God reflected in her, and although he did not know that she was, in effect, God's personal representative on earth, sent to bring about his spiritual salvation, his love for her remained pure, untouched by physical desire. All he knew was the passion and awe which her presence evoked in him. To see her, to receive her salutation constituted the highest measure of happiness he hoped for. Her death, therefore, came as a shattering blow which all but destroyed his whole world, and although he knew that so perfect a lady as she could have gone only to heaven, he felt inconsolable grief at her loss. He sought relief from his suffering in the affections of a kindly lady who took pity on him, but in so doing he lost sight of the heavenly light which had been embodied in Beatrice. And thus it happened that, as he puts it in the opening of Inferno ("Hell," the first part of *the Divine Comedy*), having lost his way in the middle of his journey through life, he found himself lost in a dark forest. It is at this point that his spiritual pilgrimage begins.

Beatrice, in *the Divine Comedy*, has been variously interpreted as representing Theology, Revelation, or Divine Wisdom. She may indeed stand for any or all of these things, but what is most important is that Dante never strips her of her identity as a person. She remains first and foremost the woman whose beauty awakened in him the promptings of a most intense spiritual love. We must never lose sight of the fact that his redemption comes as a result of a deeply felt experience and not only from the intellectual recognition of a theological truth. The recognition comes later, but even it comes as a personal experience. This order of events is as it should be, for, psychologically speaking, anything that touches us closely is bound to be felt as personal. Thus Dante's spiritual progress may illustrate a universal truth - Dante takes this much for granted - but its meaningfulness can be communicated to others only in terms of his experience of it. Consequently, it is not just any picture of Hell, Purgatory, and Paradise that we come across in *the Divine Comedy*, but the picture seen, felt, and understood by Dante. In other words, what we follow in our mind's eye is not a newsreel-like travelogue through the underworld, but Dante's progress through that world. As has been noted above, it is our sense of his personal involvement with what he encounters which makes it possible for us to identify with him and, through that identification, share his experience.

DANTE'S UNIVERSE

Whatever else it may be, *the Divine Comedy* is the record of a personal experience, and is so presented. Specifically, it is the experience of a deeply committed Christian. Now it may be belaboring the obvious to say that the Christian of the Middle Ages lived in a Christian universe, but, in the twentieth century, we need to remind ourselves of this fact if we are to understand Dante's poem. Medieval man took it for granted that the universe was a finite system created by God. It had definite physical limits, and within those limits, a specific form or structure. Viewed in its physical aspect, the universe consisted of nine concentric spheres or "heavens" having the earth as their center and surrounded by a tenth heaven called the Empyrean. Neither the earth nor the Empyrean had motion; but whereas the earth was at the center of the created universe, the Empyrean was actually outside of time and space, being the eternal, infinite realm where God, the angels, and the saved dwelt. The nine heavens, on the other hand, were constantly revolving about their center in accordance to the motion imparted to them by the outermost sphere, the Primum Mobile or Prime Mover, so designated because of its function.

Dante's cosmology follows the Ptolemaic system devised by the Ancients as interpreted in the light of Christian doctrine. The nine heavens thus correspond to the five known planets of the solar system - Mercury, Venus, Mars, Jupiter, and Saturn - with the addition of the sun and the moon (both believed to be planets), the starry sky (the eighth heaven, realm of the fixed stars), and the Primum Mobile. The sun, the moon, and the fixed stars had to be assigned moving heavens since they were all observed to move across the sky in relation to the earth - the moon by virtue of its actual revolution around the earth, the sun and the stars by virtue of the earth's revolution around the sun and rotation on its own axis. The Primum Mobile, on the other hand, was deduced or "invented" in order to account for the motion of all heavenly bodies.

So much for the physical structure of the cosmos as it was understood in the Middle Ages. But to the medieval mind the universe was not only a physical reality. According to medieval thought current in Dante's day, all physical objects had been formed out of a kind of undifferentiated primeval substance called prima materia, or prime matter. What gave form to this prime matter, giving rise to the physical universe, was, ultimately, God, in whose mind all forms were said to pre-exist. Form, then, was a spiritual principle - an "idea" or concept, if we will - which infused itself into prime matter to shape or create the physical world as we know it. Consequently, the sharp separation between mind and matter which we so readily take for granted did not exist for the men of the Middle Ages. Instead, they took it as axiomatic truth that the entire universe was as much a spiritual entity as a physical structure. In other words, the cosmos was suffused with the spirit of God. At first glance this notion might seem to smack of the hazy pantheism of the nineteenth-century romantic poets who merely felt the presence of God in Nature, but that is not the case. For the world of spirit, as conceived by the medieval mind, entailed intellectual order and discipline. It was a logical world, the logic of which was reflected in the orderly structure or hierarchy of the created world. In other words, God did not slobber over and wallow in the universe He had created; He created it in an orderly fashion, and His Spirit acted on it through clearly defined channels established by Him. Thus to each of the nine heavens corresponds one of the nine orders of angels. These angels not only regulate the motion of their heaven, but also transmit God's influence downwards to the earth. (Similarly, the constellations in the starry sky also transmit heavenly "light" earthwards.) And since each of these heavens has a specific spiritual attribute, the souls of the saved are manifested to Dante in those heavens in accordance with the quality which was dominant in their lives on earth.

FORM OF THE DIVINE COMEDY

According to the thought common in Dante's time, then, the physical order reflects and expresses the spiritual order which is the ultimate reality. Since *the Divine Comedy* professes to be an image of the whole cosmos, physical and spiritual, it, too, is structured in terms of that order. The abstract form of that order is expressed by a numerological system based on the number three, the symbol of the Trinity. This is raised to nine (3 x 3, symbol of earthly perfection, as embodied in Christ, for instance), and lifted to the level of ten (symbol of divine perfection and completeness). The poem is thus divided into three sections - *Inferno* (Hell), *Purgatorio* (Purgatory), and *Paradiso*

(Paradise) - each of which contains thirty-three cantos. This division makes for a total of ninety-nine cantos; that number is raised to 100 (10 x 10) by the addition of an extra canto in *Inferno*. Each section is likewise divided into three parts, which are subdivided into seven units (symbol of the Christian mystery). These seven are raised to nine by the addition of two other units differing in kind from the first seven, and the whole is raised to ten by the addition of yet another category on an entirely different plane of Being. The structure of the poem thus reflects the nature of the universe as it was understood in Dante's day: an orderly closed system surrounded, as it were, by God.

DIVISIONS OF PARADISO

The division just described can be readily illustrated. We have seen that Paradiso consists of nine concentric spheres surrounded by the Empyrean. Among the nine spheres one may distinguish between the planetary heavens - Moon, Mercury, Venus, Sun, Mars, Jupiter, and Saturn - and the other two - Stellar Heaven and Primum Mobile - which differ in kind. These planetary heavens, numbering seven, fall into three groups: those beneath the sun, the sun, and those above the sun. We thus have our three groups, subdivided into seven units. The addition of the Stellar Heaven and the Primum Mobile raises the number to nine, and the further addition of the Empyrean brings the total to ten.

Now this order may seem cumbersome to the modern reader, and altogether meaningless. The scheme takes on meaning, however, once one realizes that to each of the heavens corresponds a moral quality or virtue, and that these moral qualities are arranged in ascending order of excellence. One may thus group the ten heavens of Paradiso into three categories: the earth-tainted "virtues" of Inconstancy, Ambition, and Earthly Love; the cardinal or moral virtues of Prudence, Fortitude, Justice, and Temperance; and the heavenly theological virtues of Faith, Hope, and Charity. (It should be noted here that the first three are merely imperfectly realized versions of the last three.) As noted before, then, the physical structure of Paradise is conditioned by a scale of spiritual values.

PURGATORIO

Although not identical with the structure of Paradiso, the scheme of Purgatorio reveals the same principle of organization. There, corresponding to the seven Christian virtues, we find the seven deadly sins arranged in ascending order on levels or platforms circling a cone-shaped mountain, Mount Purgatory; the less severe sins are purged on the higher levels since the higher one rises on the mountain, the closer one gets to heaven. The sins are grouped into three classes, according to their nature: first, we encounter examples of perverted love - Pride, Envy, and Anger; then, examples of defective love - Sloth; and finally, examples of excessive love - Avarice, Gluttony, and Carnality or Lust. These seven circles are preceded, however, by an Antepurgatory in which linger the excommunicated and the late-repentant, and these two categories bring us to a total of nine sections. Finally, atop Mount Purgatory is found the Garden of Eden, the earthly paradise, and the earthly paradise completes the scheme by raising the number of divisions to ten.

INFERNO

An examination of Inferno will reveal the same basic principle or organization. The sins punished in Dante's Hell are divided into those resulting from incontinence, i.e., lack of control over natural appetite or desire - Lust, Gluttony, Avarice, and Anger; those resulting from violence, perversion, or brutishness - Violence; and those resulting from fraud or malice, which are subdivided into examples of simple fraud and treacherous fraud. The threefold classification is based on Aristotle and has been subdivided into seven units. But a medieval Christian Hell must also make room for sins unknown to the ancient Greeks; Dante therefore adds the categories of unbelief (the heathen and the unbaptized) and misbelief (the heretics). When, to the nine circles of Hell, we add the ante-chamber where the trimmers, rejected alike by Heaven and Hell, are punished, we have arrived at the tenfold division characteristic of all three sections of the *Divine Comedy*. There is, however, in *Inferno*, a further subdivision not found in the other two parts of the poem: the last three circles, seven, eight and nine, are so subdivided as to bring the total number of distinct places of punishment for the damned to a total of twenty-four. But this additional subdivision does not invalidate the basic classification outlined above.

THE SPIRITUAL NATURE OF THE UNIVERSE

The main point to remember from this discussion is that the topography of Hell, Purgatory, and Paradise is laid out in accordance with a scale of moral values and is, in itself, evidence of the Christian nature of the universe, each part of which bears the indelible mark of God's hand. The cosmos, for Dante, is not just so much matter arranged in space and existing in time, but also an illustration - one is almost tempted to say a demonstration - in material form of the spiritual order which presided at the creation of that world and which sustains its life.

For, as we can readily see, the universe is spiritually alive for Dante - it is the spirit of God which gave matter its form and set it in motion. The material universe is supported by an equally real world of Spirit, and both worlds stem from the Absolute Reality that is God.

MAN'S RELATION TO GOD

The main interest of *the Divine Comedy* does not bear on cosmology, however. The poem is centered on man's relation to God. Dante's picture of the universe merely helps define the moral order on which depends man's redemption. Now, generally speaking, the universe is in harmony with God's will, and if this were true of life on earth, there would be no need for redemption. As long as man did not transgress against God's will in the Garden of Eden, he retained his innocence and all was well with him. But he fell to the temptation of opposing his desire to God's command, and thereby lost his state of blessedness. His Fall, Dante suggests, was inevitable - Adam's stay in the Garden of Eden lasted all of six hours (*Paradiso*, Canto 26); the Fall, then, was apparently inherent in man's nature; a composite of spirit (the soul) and matter (the flesh). But since his Fall came as a result of temptation from the outside proffered by Satan, the hope of redemption is held out to man. (Some of the angels also fell, but as their rebellion against God was self-motivated, they have no hope of being redeemed and are condemned to dwell eternally as devils in Hell.) Christ offered himself as sacrifice to atone for man's sin, but if man is to benefit from that gift of grace, he must, to the best of his ability, bend his efforts to live according to the moral law God has established for him. If he fails to exert his moral will, he only compounds original sin and eventually joins the host of the unredeemed in Hell.

The key to man's effort to gain salvation is found in Piccarda's declaration to Dante (*Paradiso*, Canto 3) that "in (God's) will is our peace." In other words, man must strive to bring his will into harmony with the will of God. To succeed in that effort is to achieve true blessedness, and the extent to which man falls short of that goal is a measure of the distance which separates him from the Divine Presence. The bulk of mankind, Dante realizes, is apparently incapable of making this effort - it is perhaps in this light that we are to read his exclamation, upon first stepping into Hell, that he did not know death had undone so many. Those who insist on denying God's will and die unrepentant are eternally damned. Those who err but try to follow his will are assigned to Purgatory, where their souls undergo the penance which will cleanse them of their sin. Only those who steadfastly walk in the ways of the Lord go directly to Paradise, where they live in the joy of God's eternal presence. As Piccarda says, "In His will is our peace."

VIRGIL AND THE ROLE OF REASON IN MAN'S LIFE

Insofar as he is an animal, man is subject to the laws of Nature, the God-given "natural law" which regulates the life of the materially-created universe. But inasmuch as he is also possessed of an immortal soul, he comes under the rule of moral law, and it is his responsibility to submit his natural appetites and the desires of his self-centered will to the dictates of that law. He is a rational being who must exert his reason to bring his appetites and passions under control. The importance of the rational faculty as a guide for man's moral life is expressed in *the Divine Comedy* by the role of guide and mentor to Dante that the Roman poet, Virgil, fulfills. It is Virgil who, at the urging of Beatrice, has come to rescue Dante from the dark forest in which he lost his way and who leads him on his journey through

Hell and Purgatory. Only when they have reached the Garden of Eden does Virgil leave Dante, and it is at that point that Beatrice takes over. In other words, human reason (symbolized by Virgil, a pre-Christian moral poet) can light man's way to moral excellence by helping him distinguish between and understand the nature of good and evil. It can make him see the moral constitution of the world; it can explain the nature of the moral law; it can even lead him to the threshold of human perfection. It cannot, however, effect redemption: The purification of the soul and the final leap heavenward are the province of Divine Love. That is why Beatrice takes over from Virgil in the Garden of Eden, where man is restored to the perfection of his original state at the time of his creation. Only she can lead Dante through the progressive unfolding of the heavenly mysteries to the revelation of eternal truth.

Although reason's sphere of operation is limited, it is nonetheless extensive, since it covers two-thirds of Dante's journey. Here again we have evidence of the fact that it is man's, not God's, experience which holds the center of the stage in *the Divine Comedy*. Reason, according to medieval thought, was given to man to guide him through life, and it is precisely the drama of human life which is unfolded to us in *Inferno* and *Purgatorio*. The souls Dante encounters there may belong to the dead, but it is their earthly passions which have put them in these places, and it is the moral quality of their actions on earth which is at issue. Dante's vision of Hell and Purgatory is thus nothing short of an encyclopedic commentary on the morality of human actions. Such a commentary, as we have seen, is implicit in the very structure of Hell and Purgatory - a structure, incidentally, explained to Dante by Virgil, though, in Purgatory, which is structured according to Christian ideas, Virgil could not have known he, too, must seek explanation from the souls who are being purged.

But Virgil's function involves more than providing a guided tour through strange, exotic places. Dante's response to what he sees is always human: He reacts with pity, sympathy, or indignation. For that matter, it is the poet's ability to meet whatever he encounters with his total equipment as a human being - his feelings as well as his intellect - that brings his visionary world to life for us. Yet, lest his all-too-human faculties lead his judgment astray, Virgil is ever at his side to correct his view, to make sure that neither the terror nor the beauty of life distort his moral perspective.

VIRGIL AND THE IDEAL EMPIRE

Reason's role in salvation is simple: to bring man to the point where he willingly harmonizes his will with that of God. But man is a complex being who cannot usually accomplish this end single-handedly; hence he has been given institutions whose job it is to support him in his efforts. In Dante's mind these institutions are two: the Church and the State. The Church is to minister to the spiritual needs of mankind, bringing and interpreting God's word to man; the State, in the form of the Holy Roman Empire, is to insure the political stability and physical security needed for orderly human living. Strongly opposed to the secular claims of the papacy, Dante insists that both emperor and pope receive their authority directly from God; the pope's assertion of authority in temporal matters is, therefore, unfounded. He has no more right, Dante maintains, to dictate to monarchs than kings have a right to interfere with the pope's running of the Church; all that is required is that kings respect the spiritual authority of the pope as Vicar of Christ (These views were defined in Dante's treatise on the subject, the De Monarchia.)

If Dante champions the secular independence of kings and emperor, then his choice of Virgil as his guide through Hell and Purgatory is all the more appropriate. For Virgil, symbolizing Reason, also stands as the representative of an ideal of order in the secular world. His **epic**, *the Aeneid*, celebrated the Roman Empire that had just come into being under Augustus. While it dealt with the escape of Aeneas and a band of companions from Troy after the fall of that city, and traced their adventures until they settled in Italy to become the ancestors of the Romans, it was designed to praise the political stability and peaceful order of the newly founded empire. Rome's great contribution to civilization, Aeneas was told by the ghost of his father whom he met on his journey through the underworld, would be the concept of Law, the ideal of orderly government. No wonder, then, that Dante, at heart a patriot who was very much aware of Rome's legacy to Italy, should choose Virgil as his guide.

VIRGIL AND CHRISTIANITY

There is another reason which makes the choice of Virgil meaningful. Not only was Virgil the only poet of antiquity whose reputation was never completely obscured after the fall of Rome, but he was considered by the Middle Ages to have foretold the coming of Christ. In the fourth Eclogue Virgil had sung the return of the golden age of Saturn - the return of justice and universal peace - which, he said, was promised by the birth of a child. Medieval readers interpreted this poem as a **foreshadowing** of the birth of Christ, the restorer of universal peace. Consequently Virgil was seen as a great moral teacher; this prestige made him a most appropriate embodiment of the moral reason which is to guide man through life to the portals of salvation.

THE DIVINE JUSTIFICATION OF THE EMPIRE

In Virgil the moral and political **themes** of *the Divine Comedy* are united. This unity is yet another indication of the way in which the various elements of Dante's poem are held together and are seen to be so many facets of the same fundamental truth. Reason as a guide to moral truth also holds implications for the political life of the world. And political order ties in with divine truth since, as Dante tells us in the *De Monarchia*, the Roman Empire was consecrated by God himself when Christ chose to come to earth and assume his human form under the authority of that empire. (It is this argument which is the basis for Dante's contention that the emperor receives his authority, not from the pope, but directly from God.) In short, there is a divine order which is to be reflected not only in the life of the private individual, but also in the life of the body politic: hence the important place assigned to political questions in the *Divine Comedy*.

MEDIEVAL POLITICS - THE HOLY ROMAN EMPIRE AND THE PAPACY

If we wish to understand the political battle waged by Dante in his poem, we must know something of the political situation of his day. Theoretically, the Roman Empire still existed as the Holy Roman Empire of the Middle Ages. Its function was to insure the universal order which, according to Dante, was conducive to man's material well-being and his happiness on earth. Nominally, the emperor exercised his authority throughout the West; actually, the German emperors wielded little or no power outside of Germany. In Italy, the cradle of the Roman Empire, it was the papacy which became a center of political power as it extended its authority to temporal matters through the expansion of the Papal States. The rest of the country consisted of individual city-states, dukedoms, independent fiefs, and assorted principalities, all of which constantly made and broke alliances designed to protect them against encroachment from one another or from the papacy.

THE POLITICAL STRUGGLE IN FLORENCE

Generally speaking, the political life of thirteenth-century Italy oscillated between the two focal points of pope and emperor. In Florence, Dante's city, which had become a major economic and political power, there was a split between the two parties, the Guelfs and the Ghibellines. The former represented the new commercial and industrial class which gave the city its wealth and power; they supported the papacy. The Ghibellines, on the other hand, consisted of the feudal nobility whose power was being displaced by the commercial class; they naturally supported the claims of the Empire and looked north of the Alps for political and military support. It was undoubtedly the Ghibellines' tendency to seek the support of the emperor which made the Guelfs ally themselves with the pope.

Whenever one party came into power, members of the opposition were sent into exile, and their property was often confiscated. In short, Florence, like most independent communes of the time, was faction-ridden, and its history during the thirteenth century reads like a series of plots and counterplots, with power shifting back and forth between the two parties. The Guelfs were disastrously defeated at the battle of Montaperti in 1260, but Ghibelline power was definitely broken at Benevento in 1266. The final defeat of the Ghibellines did not, however, bring an end to factionalism in Florence. Two new parties arose, the Whites and the Blacks, the former following the direction marked out by the Guelfs and the latter taking up the allegiances of the Ghibellines. The struggle between the two reached a state of crisis by 1300, and the Blacks, in desperation, turned to Pope Boniface VIII for help. The pope's agent, Charles of Valois, who had been sent to Florence presumably as a peacemaker, turned the city over to the Blacks. They immediately proceeded to exile the leaders of the Whites, or institute proceedings against them; in Dante's case, they trumped up charges of graft against him, and since he refused to return to answer these charges, they condemned him to be burned at the stake if he was ever captured.

Not only did the Papacy intervene in the temporal disputes between White and Blacks in Florence, but, once it moved from Rome to Avignon (the so-called "Babylonian Captivity"), it became subservient to the political interests of the French kings. As Dante saw it, not only did the popes subject their spiritual authority to the temporal ambitions of earthly rulers and thus pervert the whole meaning of their mission, but they also contributed to the disruption of order in the social and political life of the world. The only hope was to restore the meaning of empire by having the emperor reassert his authority over Italy. It is to that purpose that Dante urged Henry VII of Luxemburg to march into Italy; it is for this reason that he rejoiced at Henry's coming; and it is why he felt such bitter disappointment when, in 1313, Henry died, having accomplished nothing.

DANTE AND FLORENCE

With Henry's death Dante lost his last hope of seeing a central authority imposed on the Christian world; he also lost his hope of ever returning to his beloved Florence. For Dante was deeply attached to his city. He may have denounced it as a fountain of iniquity, a source of corruption, and a bed-rock of depravity; but his bitter invectives in *the Divine Comedy* are an indication of his love, not his hatred for the town on the Arno. The bond which tied the men of his day to their native cities reached beyond such questions as likes or dislikes, approval or disapproval. Until well into the nineteenth century at least, man's prime allegiance was to his native town: There his ancestors had lived; there he was born and bred; there he reared his children - in short, his native town was part of himself because it was truly his home. It is this strong feeling which moves Dante when he contemplates Florence, and the more its conduct earns his condemnation, the more hurt he is by the spectacle of its life.

DANTE'S SENSE OF HIS OWN IMPORTANCE

Dante's attitude towards his city may betray a fundamental egotism in the man - anything he dislikes is automatically condemned in the light of eternal truth - but this egotism is the source of his strength and the center from which his whole poem radiates. For that matter, it is his strong sense of identity which makes *the Divine Comedy* possible. Without that sense of self the amazing movement from personal experience to general principle and universal truth would be impossible. Always, at the center, stands Dante's personal experience, and it is his faith in his own importance as an individual human being which enables him to recognize in that experience the fundamental truths which underlie all experience. Thus his exile from Florence may have provoked him to bitterness, but that bitterness is transferred to his utopian vision of universal peace, so that it is the city's interference with the moral and political order intended by God which now provokes Dante's attacks. The feeling is still intensely personal, born out of the bitterness of his experience, but the purpose is moral and the design universal.

To accuse Dante of a monstrous kind of self-centeredness, as some have done, is to miss the point. His egotism is an assertion both of the value of human beings and the meaningfulness of their experience. For if Dante Alighieri, the Florentine, is important and if his experience has meaning, then each of us is equally important, and each of us undergoes equally meaningful experiences. As we have already noted at the beginning of this essay, God's concern for Dante's salvation holds out the promise of his concern for everyone's salvation, for to God all souls are equally important.

THE POET AS TEACHER

We may all stand equal to Dante in our individuality, but few among us have the power to see as far-reachingly as he, and fewer among us are capable of sustaining and ordering the complete vision that his imagination created for him. It therefore becomes his duty to report on what he has seen, to enlighten us with the knowledge that has been imparted to him. That is the purpose of the Divine Comedy. Here again the selection of Virgil as his initial guide is significant. For Virgil is conceived of as the ideal poet, and the ideal poet is not only the creator of beautiful forms, but the moral teacher and spiritual leader of his people. As Petrarch and Boccaccio were to explain in the century after Dante, poetic fiction presented truth hidden beneath a veil of beautiful images - that veil being intended to preserve the sacredness of the truth from desecration by vulgar minds. But the inspiration which moved the poet came from God, and thus it was that the poet was truly the leader of his people. Since Virgil was the greatest poet of antiquity whose work was known to the Middle Ages, he fittingly became Dante's guide not only by virtue of his representing Reason, but also by virtue of his achievement as the author of *the Aeneid*, the national **epic** of the Romans. He is thus not only a guide, but also a source of inspiration for Dante's own **epic** undertaking in *the Divine Comedy*. Virgil, the Middle Ages, felt, had shown the Romans the truth about themselves; Dante, in his poem, intends to perform the same service for the Christian world. His vision is inspired by his love for Beatrice; his mission, on the other hand will be undertaken in the light of his admiration for the Roman poet. Guided by Virgil, instructed by Beatrice, he can return to earth and report to mankind on the love which moves the sun and the other stars - in other words, the love which is the source and end of all existence.

A few words about Dante's life and other works may prove helpful. There is actually little that is known about his life. He was born in Florence in 1265; he was schooled in the scholastic tradition of the medieval universities; and he was drawn to poetry as well as to philosophy. He was a disciple of Guido Guinizelli, founder of the idealistic school of poetry that came to be known as stilnovism, and a friend of Guido Cavalcanti, a contemporary poet important in his own right. Around 1297 Dante married Gemma Donati.

Dante was active in the political life of Florence. A member of the Whites, he nonetheless advocated an independent policy opposed to papal ambitions. He was consequently exiled on trumped-up charges in 1302; he never returned to his native city. The nearly twenty years of life left him were spent in various parts of northern Italy, as Dante sought support for his policies from princely patrons. The most outstanding among these were Can Grande della Scala, lord of Verona, on whom Dante pinned great hopes and to whom the Paradiso was, in effect, dedicated, and Guido Novello da Polenta, lord of Ravenna, where Dante died on the 13th or 14th of September, 1321.

DANTE'S WORKS

During his fifty-odd years Dante produced, in addition to *the Divine Comedy*, *the Vita Nuova* and *the Convivio*, as well as a collection of lyrics and several Latin treatises and letters. The earliest of these works, aside from the lyrics, is *the Vita Nuova*, which has been characterized as a "psychological novel in autobiographical form," and which is the record of his early passion for Beatrice. It is, in effect, a collection of poems, sonnets and odes, connected by a prose narrative, the sum of which presents the experience of spiritual rebirth undergone by the poet - hence the title, which means the "New Life." This work was probably written between 1292 and 1295.

DATE OF THE DIVINE COMEDY

Finally, the date of *the Divine Comedy* itself is uncertain. *The Vita Nuova* indicates that at the time of its composition Dante already had the scheme of the heavenwards ascent in mind. It is clear, however, if only because of its consummate maturity as a work of art, that Dante's masterpiece was written late in the poet's life. Most critics place it between 1314 and the poet's death in 1321.

THE "REAL" BEATRICE

One last word about Beatrice and her role in the poet's life. Much has been written about her, and she is usually identified with a certain Beatrice Portinari, wife of a wealthy banker, Simone dei Bardi. But to read *the Vita Nuova* as literal autobiography is to misunderstand the tradition within which Dante worked. Now he may or may not have been in love with Beatrice Protinari at some period of his life (there is, for that matter, evidence of a period of altogether riotous licentiousness in Dante's life), but the Beatrice of *the Vita Nuova* and *the Divine Comedy* is so much the creature of an idealistic literary tradition that no live model need be found to explain her. She is the donna angelicata (the "angelized" lady) of all stilnovist poets, and her function is that of all such idealized ladies: to lead her lover to God. All biographical speculation is beside the point; first and foremost, Beatrice is an ideal that becomes the instrument of the poet's salvation. It is Dante's triumph, however, that his ideal lady is to the readers of his poem a surpassingly real lady, too.

INFERNO

. . . .

A preliminary note on Dante's Hell will help the reader to visualize the over-all structure of Inferno and keep its details in their proper perspective. Hell consists of a series of nine concentric circles or regions arranged around the wall of a huge funnel; these are preceded by a kind of vestibule, or antechamber, separated from them by the river Acheron. The entrance is in the dark forest in which Dante has lost his way; the exit is at the bottom of the funnel. It is there that Satan is imprisoned in a lake of ice, and when the poets finally get past him, they come out on the underside of the world, in the hemisphere of water, at the foot of Mount Purgatory.

As we have seen in the Introduction, the physical structure of Hell corresponds to a moral hierarchy. The vestibule is reserved for the trimmers, the lukewarm or indifferent, who were neither good nor evil but cared only for themselves. The first circle, after the river Acheron, consists of Limbo, the abode of the heathen and unbaptized who led decent lives. In the next four circles are punished the sins of Incontinence: The second circle is reserved for the lustful, the third for the gluttonous, the fourth for the avaricious and prodigal, and the fifth for the wrathful. These are separated from the lower parts of Hell by the walls of the City of Dis (classical god of the underworld), surrounded by the river Styx.

The second section of Hell begins with the sixth circle, in which is punished a sin not defined by classical antiquity but necessary to the Christian world: heresy. Since it contains a group of sinners who do not come under the general categories of Incontinence, Violence, or Fraud, it is separated from the circles beneath by a sharp precipice.

The seventh circle, surrounded by the river Phlegethon, is devoted to the punishment of Violence. It is divided into three rings according to the object against which violence was directed. The first ring contains those who were violent against their fellow-man; the second, those who were violent against themselves - primarily suicides; and the third, those who were violent against God. This circle is separated from the last section of Hell by a deep abyss. There the two classes of Fraud, simple and treacherous, are punished in the eighth and ninth circles respectively.

The eighth circle, known as Malebolge (literally, Evil Pouches), is itself divided into ten rings which Dante likens to moats surrounding a fortress. The walls of these moats are connected by bridge-like passageways. Those guilty of simple fraud are thus divided into ten separate categories: 1) seducers and panders, 2) flatterers, 3) simonists, 4) soothsayers, 5) grafters, 6) hypocrites, 7) thieves, 8) evil counselors, 9) sowers of discord, 10) counterfeiters and falsifiers.

At the center of the eighth circle is a deep well, at the bottom of which is found the ninth circle known as Cocytus. There the perpetrators of treacherous fraud are punished for their sins.

This last circle, too, is subdivided. There are four sections: Caina, for the betrayers of kin; Antenora, for the betrayers of their country; Ptolomea, for the betrayers of guests; and Judecca, for the betrayers of benefactors. It is in this last section that Satan is imprisoned in a frozen lake, chewing in the mouths of his three heads the arch-traitors of mankind: Judas, Brutus, and Cassius.

INFERNO

CANTO 1–4

. . . .

CANTO 1–4

The Divine Comedy opens with Dante lost in a dark, wild wood. He was, he says, in the middle of his journey through life, and adds that the memory of the fearful night he spent in that forest is as bitter as death itself; nonetheless, in order to report on the good that was revealed to him, he will relate all that he encountered.

Dante cannot recall how he got to this forest at the bottom of a valley because, he tells us, he was too full of sleep when he abandoned what he calls the true road. Looking for a way out, he comes to the foot of a mountain, the top of which is bathed in sunlight, and tries to climb it. He cannot reach the top, however. He is first distracted by a handsome leopard, then finds his path blocked by a lion, and is finally driven back into the valley by a fierce she-wolf. Rushing downwards to escape the beast, he meets the ghost of the Roman poet, Virgil, who tells him that no one can get past that wolf, as she slays all who come her way. But, Virgil continues, if Dante is willing to follow him through Hell and up Mount Purgatory, he can be led out of the frightful valley and may hope to rise to Heaven and meet the spirits of the blessed. Dante, eager to escape from the mournful place he is now trapped in, readily accepts Virgil's offer to be his guide, and they immediately start on their journey.

CANTO 2

Although Dante has accepted Virgil's offer without hesitancy, he soon is beset with doubts as he contemplates the difficulty of the undertaking. Aeneas (the hero of Virgil's **epic**, the Aeneid, and mythical ancestor of Rome) and St. Paul (the founder of Christian theology) were permitted to descend into Hell during their lifetime, but, Dante asks, does Virgil see sufficient virtue in him to make him worthy of such an enterprise? These fears, however, are quickly allayed by Virgil, who says that he was sent expressly to lead Dante out of the forest. He was sent by none other than Dante's beloved, the fair and blessed Beatrice, who acted on instructions from the Virgin Mary transmitted to her by St. Lucy. When Dante hears of Beatrice's charity for him, he hesitates no longer. Declaring himself ready to make Virgil's will his own, Dante steps along the steep, woody path which will lead them to the gates of Hell.

Comment

The opening cantos are an imaginative presentation of Dante's spiritual state. He sets his vision in the jubilee year 1300, when he had reached the peak of his manhood at the age of 35. He knows that life is a pilgrimage of the soul on its way to God, but he has lost his way. True, he tries to get back on the right path and reach salvation (the sunbathed summit of the mountain), but his attempts are thwarted by the obstacles of Lust (the leopard), Pride (the lion), and Avarice (the she-wolf). (These three allegorical animals have also been interpreted as representing the three classifications of sin - Incontinence, Violence, and Fraud - discussed in the Introduction.) Just as Dante despairs of his state, Virgil, representing human reason, comes to rescue him. But human reason leads to worldly wisdom; as we have seen, it is not a sufficient guide to salvation. Dante hesitates, therefore, until Virgil tells him that their journey is to be undertaken under the patronage of divine wisdom (Beatrice), prompted by divine grace (the Blessed Virgin) transmitted through the illuminating grace represented by St. Lucy (the patron saint of the eyes). The sanction of this feminine trinity of divine love gives Dante the assurance to undertake the difficult journey.

The design of *the Divine Comedy* is complex, however. Dante's spiritual evolution, as we know, entails more than his growing understanding of the position of his soul in the scheme of salvation. It also involves the ever-widening perception of the eternal order which rules the life of man, of the world, and of the whole universe. Thus Beatrice is not only the woman in whom Dante loved, while she was alive, the reflected beauty and goodness of God, but she also represents Theology and Divine Wisdom. In the same way, the three animals represent not only the sins that interfere with personal salvation and the moral perfection of the world, but also contemporary political forces which, in Dante's mind stood in the way of a perfect order on earth. The leopard is thus the city of Florence; the lion, the ruling house of France; and the she-wolf the Papacy. All three, Dante felt, were upsetting the divine plan for the rule of the world by preventing the establishment of a truly universal empire which, under the Holy Roman Emperor, would regulate the temporal affairs of the world while the Church ruled over the spiritual life of mankind. This balance between emperor and pope, i.e., temporal and spiritual power, is hinted at in Dante's **allusion** to Aeneas and St. Paul.

CANTO 3

Dante reads the inscription over the Gate of Hell, which announces to all who approach it that it was set there for all time by Divine Power, Wisdom, and Love (the Holy Trinity), and calls on all who enter there to abandon hope forever. He and Virgil come into the vestibule housing the trimmers - people who, Dante says, were never alive because they lived without commitment to either good or evil. There, too, are found those angels who neither rebelled against God nor remained faithful to him, but kept to themselves. The anguish of these souls is overwhelming, for they are condemned to chase forever after a swiftly running flag, the shifting nature of which is expressive of their own wavering spirits. After his sight, Dante and Virgil come to the river Acheron, over which the souls of the damned are ferried by Charon, the boatman of the classical underworld. Dante is refused passage and, overcome by a sudden violent tremor of the ground, collapses in a dead faint.

Comment

Dante's contempt for moral equivocation is unmistakable. Because the trimmers remained passively neutral in the drama of existence, choosing neither good nor evil, they are neither damned nor saved. They can hope for nothing beyond an eternity of the aimless restlessness which is the appropriate reward for the contemptible meaninglessness of their lives.

The river Acheron and the boatman Charon are both derived from classical sources - the description of the underworld in *the Aeneid* and whatever other classical mythology was known in Dante's day. Dante borrows many features of the classical underworld for his Christian Hell.

Dante's fainting is an indication of the tremendous emotional turmoil within him as he is about to enter into Hell proper. Since he has lost his way through life, the possibility that he may rightfully belong in Hell is frighteningly real. It is this possibility which he cannot face and escapes from momentarily by fainting. His intuitive awareness that what he witnesses may apply to him personally often arouses such strong terror in him that he loses consciousness. His loss of consciousness is thus an indication of the intensity of his personal involvement in what he experiences. It is also a symbolic death which is followed by a spiritual rebirth which strengthens him; we may be sure that this pattern of growth is present whenever he faints.

CANTO 4

A heavy peal of thunder wakens Dante, whom Virgil then leads into the first circle of Hell, Limbo. Here are placed the souls of those who lived good lives but who could not achieve salvation because they had not been baptized. Their only pain is the hopelessness of ever satisfying their desire to see God. Only once, Virgil tells his companion, were some few among them saved: Christ came to bless and retrieve the souls of Adam, Noah, the Patriarchs,

Moses, King David, and others. The rest live in darkness, sighing out their hopeless desire. Amid the darkness Dante finds a circle of light, however. There he meets the great poets of antiquity - Homer, Horace, Ovid, and Lucan. These lead him to a castle where he finds the great heroes and thinkers of the ancient and heathen worlds. After a brief stay among them, the two poets move on.

Comment

The Biblical figures are important because they represent key steps in the Judeo - Christian picture of the history of mankind. It is inconceivable that divine grace should not have redeemed them since they are the designated ancestors of mankind, of the Chosen People, and of the Messiah.

Although Christian orthodoxy could not extend the same privilege to the pagan greats, they are nonetheless placed in a privileged section of Limbo because their achievement was an important element in the cultural tradition of the medieval Christian world. As we have seen, the classification of sins in Hell is based on Aristotle, whom Dante here refers to simply as "the master of those who know."

INFERNO

CANTO 5-8

. . . .

CANTO 5

Here Dante comes to the beginning of what is properly the Christian Hell. He descends into the second circle, where he first encounters Minos, the Infernal Judge of the classical world, who examines each sinner and assigns him his proper circle for punishment by making the appropriate number of circles with his tail. Here, too, are found the souls of the lustful, whose sin it was to subject the rule of reason to their appetites. They are blown about continually in darkness by a violent wind, and they shriek, wail, and blaspheme God as they come near a cleft in the ground which was formed by an earthquake at the time of the Crucifixion. This cleft stands as a perpetual reminder of the salvation they have lost. Virgil points out many famous lovers in the whirlwind, but Dante asks to speak to one pair in particular who always keep together in the storm.

As the souls in question stop to speak with him, Dante learns that they are Paolo and Francesca, the famed lovers of Rimini. Francesca, daughter of the ruler of Ravenna, was married off to the deformed son of the lord of Rimini. She fell in love with her brother-in-law Paolo, however, and when her husband discovered them together, he killed them on the spot. Such was their love, however, that even in Hell they cannot be separated, and Paolo always keeps by Francesca's side.

Having heard this much from Francesca, Dante asks her how the passion which was her undoing swept over her. She tells him that one day she and Paolo sat together reading the romance of Lancelot and Guinevere, wife of King Arthur. The story of that love prompted their own feelings, but only when they came to Lancelot's kiss were they overcome: Paolo kissed her and, in Francesca's words, "that day we read no further." Paolo's spirit weeps during Francesca's narration, and Dante is so moved with pity for the lovers that he faints and falls as if dead.

Comment

The cleft produced by the earthquake which accompanied the Crucifixion appropriately belongs in the second circle not only because that circle marks the beginning of the Hell where Christian sins are punished, but also because the lustful abandoned the spirit for the flesh, and it was in the flesh that Christ suffered on the Cross.

The story of Paolo and Francesca, already a well-known legend in Dante's day, is Dante's tribute to the beauty of courtly love (the medieval system of adulterous, romantic love). He recognizes its deep seated human quality and sympathizes with the force of longing which keeps the lovers together even in

Hell - not even death can separate them. But for all his sympathy and pity, Dante does not lose his moral bearings: He puts the lovers squarely in Hell, consigning them to an eternity of agitation similar to the restlessness of their passion. Romantic passion is an assertion of private will against the moral order of the world; the lovers never knew the secret revealed to Dante by Piccarda in *Paradiso:* "in His will is our peace." Consequently, having misconstrued the true nature of love, which is spiritual, and having put their will before that of God, no peace can ever be theirs.

Here again, Dante's collapse is significant. It is due not only to his strong sympathy and pity for the lovers and their fate, but also to his strong identification with them. In other words, he recognizes himself in them (Beatrice will upbraid him in the Garden of Eden for having strayed from the path of pure love), and that recognition is more than he can bear. For it is by virtue of his being human that he associates himself with the pathos of Paolo and Francesca's situation. The thought that their love - for it is love, after all, that moved them - is to be condemned is more than he can face up to. If they are guilty through love then, he too, may be found guilty. His loss of consciousness is thus a measure of his limited human vision; Beatrice, we may be sure, would not have fainted at the sight of the lovers of Rimini.

CANTO 6

When Dante recovers, he finds he has been transported to the third circle, where the Gluttonous are punished. An unvarying storm of hail, foul water, and snow pours down on the souls placed there, and from the ground rises a putrid smell. Standing over them, the three-headed dog Cerberus (guardian of the underworld in the *Aeneid*) barks at them and tears them to pieces. Finally, Dante tells us, the incessant rain makes the spirits imprisoned there howl like dogs.

As Dante and Virgil step along, placing their soles, as Dante puts it, on the emptiness of the spirits which only appear to have bodies, they are stopped by the ghost of a Florentine nicknamed Ciacco (Pig). Ciacco predicts the outcome of the struggle between White and Blacks in Florence; the Blacks will triumph for a long time. As for the cause of civil strife, Ciacco ascribes it to pride, envy, and avarice. Only two among the Florentines are just, but no one listens to them. Dante then asks about the fate of certain prominent citizens, and Ciacco tells him he will meet them further down in Hell. Lastly, Ciacco asks to be recalled to the memory of the living; he then falls back down on the ground.

Virgil comments at this point that Ciacco shall rise no more until the Last Judgment, when all souls shall revisit their graves and resume their flesh. Dante wishes to know if their suffering will be greater then, and Virgil refers him to Aristotle ("thy science") as incorporated in Thomas Aquinas: The more perfect a thing is, the more it feels pleasure and pain. As they reach the next descent, they encounter Plutus, the ancient god of riches.

Comment

This canto contains the first of several condemnations of Florence for its divisions and anarchic political life. In five lines Ciacco sums up the main political events of 1300–1302.

The souls of the dead have the appearance, but not the substance, of human bodies; that is why Dante can step right through them as he crosses the third circle. Since Aquinas says that the soul without the body does not have the perfection of its nature, and since Virgil reminds Dante of the resurrection of the flesh on Judgment Day, his answer to Dante's question about the torments of the damned after the Last Judgment is clear: They will indeed suffer greater pain.

CANTO 7

"Pape Satan, pape Satan aleppe" - with these strange words Plutus voices his rage and amazement at the sight of Dante and Virgil. But Virgil's sharp answer makes him collapse and fall to the ground. The two poets then move into the fourth circle. This circle is divided into two halves, one housing the avaricious, among whom Dante notices many churchmen, and the other containing the prodigal. The two groups are condemned to rolling massive weights with their chests; they move these towards one another until they meet and clash. Taunting each other with their sins - "why do you keep?" and "why do you spend?" - they turn around until they meet again at the other half of the circle. Virgil then explains to Dante the nature of Fortune: Her function, assigned to her by God, is constantly to redistribute wealth among the peoples.

The poets then descend to the next circle, the fifth, reserved for the wrathful. This consists of a marsh formed by a streamlet and called Styx. In the mud are set the souls of the wrathful, still angry, who strike at one another, not only with their hands, but with their heads, their chests, and their feet, tearing each other with their teeth. Beneath the surface lie the sullen, who gurgle words describing their fate. Circling the marsh, the poets come to the wall of a high tower.

Comment

Plutus' words have caused much speculation and ingenious guessing. The fact remains that no one knows what they mean, if anything at all. It is best to think of them as a sub-human attempt at human language on the part of a demon, and an expression of his anger and astonishment at the sight of a living man.

In Dante's Hell, as in Puratory, the punishment always fits the crime. Therefore the angry act out their anger against one another. The sullen, on the other hand, retain their negative passivity as they stay submerged beneath the surface of the bog, their words gurgling in their throats.

CANTO 8

Before reaching the tower, the poets notice two flames rising like signals from its top; these are answered by a third far away, and soon Phlegyas is seen moving swiftly and angrily across the marsh in a boat. Ruler of the fifth circle, he thinks another soul has come to his domain, but Virgil tells him that he is only to ferry them to the entrance to the City of Dis (or Pluto, classical lord of the underworld). Dante's weight makes the boat sink lower into the waters, and this causes one soul to arise and ask for the identity of the man who comes to Hell before his death. Dante in turn asks for his name, and the questioner answers by saying that he is one who weeps. At this point Dante recognizes him (he is Filippo Argenti, and arrogant Florentine) and instead of responding to Argenti's obvious plea for sympathy, curses him. Argenti stretches out his hands to the boat but Virgil, throwing him off with angry contempt, praises Dante for his sharp answer to the arrogant sinner. He further promises Dante that his wish to see Argenti dipped in the swill will be fulfilled.

Shortly thereafter the other angry souls pull Argenti down and tear him to pieces with such fury that Dante praises and thanks God for their action.

When the poets reach the City of Dis, they find their entrance barred by a host of spirits, the fallen angels, who lock the gates against the two.

Comment

Dante's brutal treatment of Filippo Argenti, his cruel rejection of the sinner's plea for sympathy, and his sadistic delight in his torture have puzzled and shocked many readers. So has Virgil's smug approval of Dante's behavior. It has been suggested that personal vindictiveness against the arrogant, violent man who destroyed the peace of Florence lies behind the poet's anger. But such an explanation does not lessen the ugliness of Dante's conduct. Unsympathetic readers therefore point to this **episode** as proof of the poet's arrogant pride. Those wishing to defend him on the other hand, justify his actions by maintaining that they are in accordance with divine justice: It is wrong, they say, to condemn Dante for associating himself with God's hatred of sin.

Such commentators forget that God hates sin, but not the sinner. Besides, Dante is not God. He is a man, and as such he has no business making himself the dispenser of divine justice, especially at this early stage of his spiritual pilgrimage. Besides there is no place for anger in justice, and Dante is a very angry man here. There is, without a doubt, a great deal of personal venom behind his outburst. And if Dante's callous self-righteousness proves anything, it is that his understanding of the divine order is still very limited. Just as his pity for Paolo and Francesca was excessive, so, here, his anger is out of proportion.

In each case his reaction is intensely personal; with Paolo and Francesca it is the imperfection of his own love which causes him to faint, and with Filippo Argenti it is his own pride and anger which motivate his violent reaction. (Dante is fully aware of his shortcomings: In *Purgatorio* XIII he declares that he will have to do penance for envy and pride.)

One must not forget that the purpose of Dante's journey in *the Divine Comedy* is to give him the knowledge that will enable him to perfect his spiritual state. His behavior to Filippo Argenti thus not only shows him to be human and, therefore capable of morally ugly reactions, but also indicates how far he still has to go before the purification of his soul is complete. Those who condemn him make the mistake of confusing the hero of the poem with its author:

Dante the author has no illusions about the spiritual state of Dante the pilgrim, moving on his journey through Hell. As for Virgil's equally distasteful approbation of Dante's callousness, it is an indication of the fact that human reason can also fail because it, too, is limited in its perception of truth. When all is said and done, Virgil is not one of the elect.

INFERNO

CANTO 9-12

. . . .

CANTO 9

At the end of the preceding canto Virgil had tried to negotiate with the demons who barred the two poets from the City of Dis. His efforts were unsuccessful, and he returns to where Dante was left waiting. He seems disturbed, and the broken, perplexed words he speaks only heighten Dante's fear. Suddenly the three Furies of classical mythology appear over the wall, holding the head of Medusa, the sight of which turns men to stone. Virgil shields Dante from the sight. Finally, the angel whom Virgil had been expecting arrives and, chasing the demons away, opens the gates for the poets. Inside is the sixth circle, a wide plain covered with flaming tombs. Within the tombs lie the souls of the heretics and their followers.

Comment

The wall of the City of Dis marks the beginning of the second section of Hell. It also marks the separation between two kinds of sins: those due to lack of control over natural appetites (punished in Upper Hell) and those caused by the perversion of moral values. In other words, Dante and Virgil are about to move from the realm of excess to the realm of evil. And because human reason cannot ultimately comprehend evil, Virgil is unable to force his way through the gate. Only with divine help can the poets make their way into the infernal city; they must, therefore, await the arrival of God's angel. (This is the only time that Virgil is unable to overcome demonic resistance to their journey through Hell.) Here again we have evidence of the limitations of human reason, which can take man so far but no further.

CANTO 10

As the two poets make their way by the flaming tombs, a voice addresses Dante. It is Farinata degli Uberti, a leader of the Florentine Ghibellines, who rises waist - high above his tomb and asks for Dante's identity. Upon learning it, he remarks that twice he sent Dante's ancestors into exile. Dante replies that each time the Guelfs returned, but that the Ghibellines have not learned how to do so.

At this point they are interrupted by another ghost, that of Cavalcante Cavalcanti, father of Dante's close friend and fellow poet, Guido Cavalcanti. He wants to know why his son is not with Dante, and Dante explains that he is not in Hell through his own power but with the help of Virgil, whom Guido always disdained. Dante's use of the past tense makes Cavalcanti assume that his son has died, and he falls back into the tomb, aggrieved.

Farinata and Dante then resume their conversation. The Ghibelline chief tells Dante that he, too, will shortly learn how difficult the art of returning from exile is. He then asks why the

Florentines so hate him and his descendants, and Dante tells him it is because of the slaughter at the battle of Montaperti (1260 - the Guelfs were utterly defeated). When Farinata adds that he alone prevented the Ghibellines from razing Florence to the ground, Dante shifts to another question which has puzzled him: How is it that the dead in Hell have knowledge of the future, but not of the present? (This question was prompted by Cavalcanti's ignorance of his son's condition.) Farinata answers that God allows them some crude knowledge of distant events, but permits them to know nothing of the present; thus, on Judgment Day, when time comes to a stop and merges with eternity, they will be left in utter darkness. Dante now understands and asks Farinata to tell the grieving Cavalcanti that his son is still alive.

As the poets leave Farinata's tomb, Dante wears a puzzled expression. He is bewildered by Farinata's prediction about his future, and Virgil tells him to store it in his mind for the time being. When he meets Beatrice, the course of his life will be disclosed to him.

Comment

Despite his position as a heretic and leader of the Ghibellines, Farinata is treated with a certain respect by Dante. It is undoubtedly because he saved Florence from total destruction that Dante endows him with a somewhat impressive nobility and strength of character. It is the patriot in Dante who respects Farinata.

Dante's future is not actually revealed to him by Beatrice. It is she, however, who induces Dante to question his ancestor Cacciaguida about his future (*Paradiso*, Canto 17).

CANTOS 11

Crossing the sixth circle, the poets come to a rocky precipice, at the edge of which stands a monument containing a heretical pope. The smell that rises from the circles below is so pungent that they must pause behind that monument in order to accustom their senses to it. While there, Virgil explains the divisions of Hell - incontinence above the City of Dis, and "malice," or evil, below. He then tells Dante how Hell is further subdivided into its many categories of sin. Finally, in answer to Dante's question of why usury is offensive to God, he refers to both Aristotle and Genesis to account for the sinfulness of the practice.

Comment

The division of Hell has been discussed in the Introduction and summarized at the beginning of the section on *Inferno*. Here Dante classifies the sins under the headings of Incontinence, Bestiality, and Malice - these correspond to Incontinence, Violence, and Fraud. But he also first distinguishes between Upper and Lower Hell. This distinction is explained in the Comment to Canto 9.

Usury was strongly condemned by the medieval Church, and Dante would undoubtedly place all our bankers in the third ring of the seventh circle, reserved for the violent against God, Nature, and Art. (Art refers to human activities directed by human reason.) Virgil explains that Nature takes its laws from God, and that Art follows Nature, thus becoming, so to speak, a grandchild of God. According to God's words in Genesis, Virgil continues, man was ordered to replenish the earth and to earn his bread by the sweat of his brow. But the usurer, who does neither, violates God's command. He is a parasite, living off other men's work: He neither replenishes the earth (he is not a farmer) nor works for his living. He therefore does violence to Nature and to Art, and stands opposed to God's law.

CANTO 12

A steep, rocky path leads to the seventh circle, but the passage is blocked by the Cretan Minotaur, half human, half bull. Virgil's words to the monster reduce it to impotent rage, and the poets seize the opportunity to get through the passageway. The path is full of loose rocks which give way under Dante's weight, and Virgil tells him that they are a result of the earthquake which accompanied the Crucifixion. Next is the river of Blood, Phlegethon, which surrounds the seventh circle and forms its first division. Those who have committed violence against others are punished in it; they are immersed in the boiling river at different depths, according to the degree of their violence on earth. Centaurs, armed with bows and arrows, see to it that the sinners remain at their assigned depths. Their chief, Chiron, appoints a centaur to guide the two poets to a shallow part of the river where they can cross; on the way, tyrants, murderers, ruthless warriors, and highwaymen are pointed out to them.

Comment

According to ancient myth, Pasiphae, wife of Minos, king of Crete, fell in love with a bull and copulated with it by placing herself inside a hollow statue of a cow. She then gave birth to the Minotaur, whom her husband imprisoned in the Labyrinth. The Minotaur was fed a yearly tribute of youths and maidens, among whom were fourteen Athenians. He was finally put to death by Theseus, son of the king of Athens: Ariadne, daughter of Minos, fell in love with Theseus and gave him a sword with which to kill the monster, and a spool of thread to help him find his way out of the Labyrinth. Since the Minotaur's very existence does violence to all that is natural, it is appropriate that he should be guarding the entrance to the seventh circle, where the violent are punished. Similarly, the Centaurs, being half men and half horses, are appropriate expressions of the nature of this circle, where those who have perverted reason to the use of beastiality are punished.

INFERNO

CANTOS 13–18

....

CANTO 13

Having forded the boiling river, Dante and Virgil come to the second ring of the seventh circle, the wood of the suicides. The souls of those guilty of suicide have become stunted trees with withered leaves and branches; instead of fruit, they produce poison. The Harpies, obscene birds with human necks and faces, make their nests among the trees. At Virgil's bidding, Dante breaks off a small branch from a great thorn; it begins to bleed and cry out to him in pain and anguish. It is Pier delle Vigne (ca. 1190–1249), minister of the emperor Frederick II, who, having lost the confidence of his master, was imprisoned and killed himself. He further explains that the souls of suicides, having been consigned to the seventh circle, fall to the ground and sprout into trees, which the Harpies feed on. Even on Judgment Day they will not have their bodies restored to them or resume their natural shape. Since they voluntarily severed themselves from their bodies, those bodies will merely be hung upon the trees.

Two spirits suddenly rush through the wood, chased by hellhounds. They are Lano and Jacomo da Saint'Andrea, both of whom had wasted their substance and had come to an untimely end. (The waste of their substance, their means of livelihood, is a form of suicide.) Jacomo hides behind a bush, but is nonetheless caught by the hounds who tear him to pieces and carry him off. The bush, rent by the violence, bemoans its suffering and asks Dante and Virgil to gather up its fallen leaves and place them at its foot. The soul identifies itself as a Florentine who had hanged himself in his house.

CANTO 14

Dante's love for his city is such that he cannot leave before collecting the scattered leaves and restoring them to the bush. He is then led by Virgil to the third ring of the seventh circle, a plain of burning sand on which rains a shower of fire. Here are punished those who have done violence against God, Arts and Nature. The first lie on their backs - they are the least numerous, but theirs is the greatest suffering. The second group sit crouched up; the third move about without stopping. Among the first Dante notices Capaneus, one of the seven kings who besieged Thebes and who was noted for his defiance of the gods. Here, in Hell, he still remains proudly defiant. His stubborn pride, Virgil tells him, however, actually punishes him far more than the shower of fire.

Continuing to circle the burning sand by following the edge of the wood, Dante and Virgil come upon a crimson stream which crosses the burning sands; a tributary of Phelgethon, its banks are stone and it quenches the rain of fire above it. The poets will follow its banks as they cross the third ring of the seventh circle, for they will thus be sheltered from the heat and flames, but first Virgil discourses on the rivers of Hell. In Crete, Virgil tells Dante, within Mount Ida, stands an old man who, his back to the East, faces toward Rome. His head is made of gold, his chest and arms of silver, the rest of his torso of bronze, and his legs of iron, except that the right foot, on which he rests more than on the other, is made of baked clay. Every part except the gold has a fissure that drops tears. The tears drop into Hell, where they form Acheron, Styx, and Phlegethon. Finally, they drop to the bottom and form Cocytus, the ninth circle. Virgil identifies the river of Blood as Phlegethon and further informs Dante that he will find the river Lethe at the top of Mount Purgatory.

Comment

The Old Man of Crete is an allegory of the human race modeled on the ancient myth according to which there had been four "ages" of mankind: a golden, silver, bronze, and iron age. Only the golden age was perfect; each subsequent age was a falling off from the previous one. That is why the gold head is not rent by a fissure. The iron and clay feet are generally interpreted as representing secular and spiritual authority, with the latter holding more weight since the supposed "Donation of Constantine" (a medieval forgery according to which the emperor Constantine had turned the rule of Italy over to the popes). This allegorical figure is placed in Crete probably because, according to Virgil's *Aeneid* (III, 104–105), it was in Crete that the Trojan race first came into being, and the Trojans are thought to be the ancestors of the Romans. Finally, he faces towards Rome because Roman civilization succeeded the civilization of the East.

CANTO 15

The two poets move alongside the stream, sheltered from the heat and fire by walking on one of the banks. Dante is recognized by one of a group of souls walking in the fiery sand; it is Brunetto Latini, a Florentine Guelf who was a leading political figure of his city. Brunetto prophecies a glorious career for Dante; he also predicts Dante's forthcoming difficulties at the hands of the Florentines. Dante then expresses his gratitude to the man from whom he has learned how man may immortalize himself. Lastly, Brunetto names some of his sodomite companions - all clerics and scholars, and commends his book, the Treasure, to Dante's memory.

Comment

Sodomy - i.e., homosexuality - does violence to nature because it is a perversion of the natural order. Brunetto Latini was the author of an encyclopedic work, the *Livre dou Tresor*, written in French, and a didactic Italian poem, *the Tesoretto* ("Little Treasure"), which condensed much of the matter of the larger work. The latter was written in the form of an allegory, and *the Divine Comedy* shows its influence. It is this influence which Dante probably has in mind when he refers to Brunetto as his teacher; Brunetto showed him how man can make himself immortal through his work.

CANTO 16

Dante and Virgil have come within earshot of the stream's fall into the next circle when three souls, recognizing Dante as a

Florentine by his dress, leave another group and approach him. They are Guido Guerra, Tegghiaio Aldobrandi, and Jacopo Rusticucci, all prominent Florentines. Having heard from a recent arrival in their circle that the city is not happy, they eagerly question Dante about the condition of Florence. Dante, full of sorrow for their fate, tells them that newcomers with no real love for the city, coupled with Florence's too quickly acquired wealth, have fostered pride and lack of moderation in the city. The three Florentines take the news in, ask Dante to speak of them when he returns to the world of the living, and swiftly rejoin their group.

By now the two poets have reached the edge of the abyss. Virgil takes a cord which Dante wears about his waist and drops it into the abyss. At the signal, the monster Geryon floats up through the air to take them to the circle below.

CANTO 17

Geryon, the image of Fraud, appears. His face is mild and kindly, like that of a just man; his body is that of a reptile, with two hairy limbs; his tail is forked and poisonous like a scorpion's. Virgil remains with him and sends Dante to view the last class of sinners punished in the third ring of the seventh circle— the usurers who have done violence to Nature and Art (see COMMENT to Canto 11). Dante finds them sitting on the burning sand, crouched up and crying, each with a money-bag bearing armorial insignia hanging from his neck. Having observed their condition, Dante returns to Virgil; the poets climb on the monster's back and begin the circling descent through the air.

Comment

Geryon is a figure of classical mythology. According to medieval tradition, he lured strangers into his power and then secretly killed them. It is this legend which accounts for his position as guardian of the last major division of Hell, that set aside for the punishment of Fraud.

CANTO 18

While circling down the abyss on Geryon's back, Dante had the opportunity to observe the outlines of the lowest section of Hell (see the preliminary observations at the beginning of the outline of *Inferno*). The eighth circle, known as Malebolge (Evil Pouches), consists of ten concentric trenches across which run cliffs leading from the outer edge of the circle to the central well which leads to the ninth circle. It is on these cliffs that the poets walk; it is from there that they observe the punishment of the sinners in the trenches. The eighth circle is for the punishment of those guilty of simple fraud.

In the first trench Dante finds seducers and panders, who form two columns moving in opposite directions while they are lashed by horned demons. He recognizes one among the throng, Venedico de' Caccianemici, a Bolognese Guelf who had pandered his sister Ghisola to the marquess of Este. Virgil then points out Jason, the classical hero who brought back the golden fleece to Greece. He is being punished for having seduced Hypsipyle and then abandoning her with child.

The poets then turn their attention to the next trench, containing the flatterers. Their punishment is to be submerged in a pool of human excrement.

INFERNO

CANTOS 19–24

....

CANTO 19

The third trench contains the simonists, those who, buying and selling spiritual offices, prostitute the things of God. They are cast head first into round holes so that only their feet, and part of their legs show; flames of varying intensity according to the degree of their guilt burn their feet. Dante spies one flame burning more brightly than the others. When Dante asks Virgil who that is, his guide offers to carry him into the trench so that he may question the soul directly. It turns out to be Pope Nicholas III who, hearing a voice, thinks it is his successor, Boniface VIII. When he discovers his error, he explains that he is awaiting Boniface, who is due to take his place at the mouth of the hole, while he falls inside. He further predicts that Boniface will then be succeeded by Pope Clement V, because the latter will make the Church a tool of French policy. Dante bursts out with indignation at the simonists, who pervert God's order on earth; Virgil then carries him to the edge of the next trench.

Comment

Simony is more hateful than flattery to Dante because it debases the purity of God's power by turning it to material ends. Popes are Vicars of Christ: They of all people should be totally above worldly ambition. Hence their crime is all the greater.

Dante ingeniously manages to get all three popes into Hell by having Nicholas (1277–1280) predict the punishment of Boniface (1294–1303) and Clement (1305–1314). The latter, elected pope through the influence of the French king, removed the Papal See from Rome to Avignon, where it remained until 1377. It is this period in the history of the Papacy which is known as the Babylonian Captivity.

CANTO 20

The fourth trench contains the soothsayers, who tried to penetrate the secrets of the future, which belongs only to God. They file by, silently weeping, their heads so twisted that they face backwards. This disfiguration of the human form forces them to walk backwards, too, since they cannot see what is in front of them. Again, Virgil identifies various members of the throng, among whom are Amphiaraus, Tiresias, and Manto. The last named leads Virgil to discuss the origin of his native city, Mantau. A few more soothsayers are identified, and then the poets make their way to the next trench.

Comment

The soothsayers, who sought a foresight that was forbidden, are appropriately punished by being deprived, quite literally, of anything but hindsight. They distorted the universal order, and are now themselves distorted in their human form. The concreteness of Dante's vision is strikingly illustrated by his observation that their tears flow down to where their buttocks divide.

Amphiaraus was the prophet of Argos; Tiresias was a Theban prophet, and Manto was his daughter.

CANTO 21

Grafters, who made use of their public offices and authority to gain money, are punished in the fifth trench of Malebolge. They lie in boiling pitch and are torn to pieces by demons called Malebranche (Evil Claws) whenever they rise above the surface. The trench is so dark that at first Dante can see nothing but the boiling pitch. A demon then arrives, carrying a senator from the city of Lucca, and throws him down; as he rises to the surface, others, who had been hidden beneath the bridge which crosses the trench, rush at him and pierce him with prongs to teach him how to swim in the pitch. The Malebranche, catching sight of Virgil and Dante, threaten them. Virgil speaks to their chief, Malacoda, however, and the threats cease. Malacoda tells Virgil that since the cliff he is following collapsed into the sixth trench 1266 years earlier (in other words, at the time of the earthquake which accompanied the Crucifixion), he will be unable to continue his journey that way. There is another path which does bridge the sixth trench, he tells Virgil, and he offers an escort of demons to show him the way. Dante is naturally frightened by such an escort and would rather do without it, but Virgil calms his fears and they proceed on their way.

Comment

Just as the Centaurs, symbols of violence, keep the homicides in the river of Blood (Canto 12), so the Malebranche, whose name, Evil Claws, is expressive of the sin they punish, keep the grafters in the boiling pitch. The Malebranche hide from view just as their victims hid their crimes from the eyes of the world.

The Malebranche are fraudulent, and Malacoda deceives Virgil when he tells the poet that there is another path which crosses the sixth trench. (See below, Canto 23.) It may be surprising that Virgil should be taken in by the lie, but since graft is a hidden fraud, secretly perpetrated, human reason is not always able to detect the deceit. Consequently, Virgil does not doubt the demon's words.

CANTO 22

The escort had gotten under way at the end of the preceding canto with a trumpeting blast caused by the leader's breaking wind. Dante now wryly comments on the exotic horn which set them under way. Marching along, he notices that the grafters will occasionally sneak relief from their torment by arching their backs over the surface of the pitch. He also observes that many will lie, like frogs in ditchwater, with only their mouths protruding; as soon as they spy the demons, they dive back beneath the surface. One of them, however, did not move quickly enough; he is caught by a demon's hook and lifted to the top of the cliff, where he is immediately set upon by the other fiends. At Dante's request, Virgil questions him. He identifies himself as one Ciampolo, who had been in the service of King Thibault of Navarre. The leader of the escort keeps his fellow fiends off while Virgil questions Ciampolo further, but the demons itch to get at the poor sinner and keep taking swipes at him. Ciampolo outwits his tormentors, however. He promises to bring seven other sinners to the surface, and while the demons take up positions along the cliff to hook those seven as soon as they appear, he jumps back into the boiling pitch. Infuriated at having lost their victim, two of the demons start a brawl which lands them in the boiling tar. While their fellows are busy rescuing them, Dante and Virgil move on.

Comment

The farcical humor of the situation is unmistakable and certainly deliberate on Dante's part. The demons, who represent the sin, are outsmarted by the sinner because they are stupidly short-sighted and greedy; the scene in Hell reproduces the comedy of petty self-interest, deceit, and double-dealing which is part of the life of any bureaucracy. The spectacle is a real farce because it is essentially stupid: The seeker of favors and the influence - peddler inevitably fall into someone else's trap. Dante, following the medieval tradition which staged devils as comic figures, uses humor to point up the moral.

CANTO 23

Dante, meditating on what he has just witnessed, is reminded of the fable of the Frog and the Mouse. He becomes fearful lest the demons seek revenge for their mishap, and surely enough, he suddenly sees them coming at him and Virgil with outstretched wings. But before the Malebranche can seize them, Virgil takes Dante in his arms and glides down into the next trench, the sixth. There they come upon the hypocrites, who walk about slowly, weighed down by gilded cloaks of lead. Two friars of Bologna, Catalano and Loderingo, speak with Dante. They had been chosen by the Florentines to rule their city jointly in order to restore peace, but failed in their task.

Dante is about to tell them what he thinks of their evil when he notices one spirit, transfixed to the ground in the form of a cross, over whom the other hypocrites walk. It is the high-priest of the Hebrews, Caiaphas, who had advised the Council that Christ should be killed for the good of the nation. His father-in-law, Annas, and other members of the Council who supported his views are similarly punished.

Virgil then asks Catalano the way out of the trench. He is told that he will shortly come upon the ruins of the other bridge across the sixth trench; he and Dante can climb upon the rocks and reach the top of the ledge. Virgil is angered when he remembers that Malacoda had told him that that bridge was intact; he realizes he has been deceived. But as they have no alternative, he and Dante proceed to where they must climb the cliff.

Comment

The fable alluded to by Dante illustrates the point made in the Comment to Canto 22: A mouse asks a frog to ferry it across a river. The frog agrees, but betrays the mouse and tries to pull it down to the bottom. While they are struggling, a hawk spots them, catches them, and eats them both. (In one version of the fable the mouse actually escapes.)

CANTO 24

Because Virgil seems troubled at the deceit perpetrated by Malacoda, Dante is thrown into despair; he realizes once again how totally dependent he is on his guide. When Virgil perceives Dante's anxiety, he smiles reassuringly, and his smile calms Dante just as it had calmed him at their first meeting. They now begin the difficult ascent, Virgil helping Dante and pulling him up. When they reach the top, Dante is exhausted and out of breath; he sits down to rest, but his companion reminds him of the great things that await him beyond the difficult journey through Hell, and Dante rises to his feet again. He keeps talking as they walk on to cover up any sign of faint-heartedness.

When they come to the seventh trench, they find it filled with thieves who are attacked by horrible serpents. One of them is suddenly pierced at the base of the neck by a serpent; he immediately catches fire, burns to ashes, and is then restored to his human shape again. It is Vanni Fucci. When Dante expresses surprise at his not being among the violent, Fucci explains that he has been sent here because he robbed the treasure of a sacristy. Fucci is so much ashamed at having been discovered by Dante that he foretells the disasters that will lead to Dante's exile, just to spite the poet.

Comment

Dante's despair, his exhaustion after climbing out of the hypocrites' den, indicate once again that what is at stake is the state of his soul. What he has just witnessed has personal relevance. Dante had held public office in Florence - he was exiled on trumped-up charges of graft, and the sight of those who used public office for private gain must have been exceedingly unpleasant to him. Dante was not a grafter, but no one holding public office can altogether avoid the corruption that is part and parcel of political life. He cannot therefore have been altogether immune from small faults; that is why he is so uneasy when the

Malebranche offer to escort him and Virgil on their way past the fifth trench. Human reason cannot completely withstand the pressures of political life; consequently Virgil could be deceived by the Malebranche. And Dante's fears that the demons may yet catch him in their power certainly suggest that his conscience is not altogether clear in this area.

When the charge of graft is leveled against one, especially when it is essentially unjustified, the only way out that reason can suggest is to make oneself out to be altogether pure. Complete purity, however, is rarely achieved by man. Nonetheless, it is natural and reasonable that the accused should take refuge in a somewhat "holier-than-thou" attitude. But such an attitude is already a form of hypocrisy - making oneself out to be better than one is; that is why it is among the hypocrites that Virgil seeks refuge from the Malebranche. It is no wonder, then, that the ascent from their trench is so difficult.

The point becomes even clearer if we contrast the difficulty of that ascent with the easy exit from the trench of the simonists (Canto 19). There, too, Dante had left the cliff; but that was at the invitation of Virgil, to satisfy his curiosity.

Here, on the other hand, the descent among the hypocrites was a means of escape from another sin. It is no accident, therefore, that Dante has to climb on the ruins of the bridge which collapsed at the time of the Crucifixion. Christ died on the Cross to redeem mankind, and Dante needs to be reminded of this fact when he comes dangerously close to undoing Christ's sacrifice by losing his own path to salvation - in other words, by sinning. The fact that it is human reason (Virgil) that has put him in his precarious position only increases his anxiety and adds to his exhaustion.

INFERNO

CANTOSX 25–30

....

CANTO 25

At the conclusion of his angry prophecy, Fucci directs an obscene gesture at God. Serpents, whom Dante will henceforth consider friends, coil about the thief and he flees. Next, Cacus rushes by, a Centaur guilty of theft, laden with snakes and topped by a fire-throwing dragon. Then Dante witnesses a horrifying scene. Three Florentines, Agnello, Buoso, and Puccio, come by. One of them asks where a fourth, Cianfa, has gone to. No sooner has the question been asked than a six-footed serpent rushes up, clasps one of them and bites his face. The serpent, which is none other than Cianfa, has attached itself to Agnella, and a frightful metamorphosis takes place as the two merge into one body resembling neither serpent nor human being. When the fusion is completed, the resultant monstrous creature walks languidly away.

It is now Buoso's turn. A small serpent pierces his navel, then lies down on the ground and gazes at him. Buoso, suddenly overcome with fatigue, yawns and gazes back. Slowly, step by step, another metamorphosis takes place: Buoso and the serpent (Francesco, a fifth Florentine) gradually exchange bodies. When this transformation is completed, the new serpent, Buoso, flees hissing along the valley, and Francesco follows, muttering and spitting at it.

Comment

The serpent robbed man of his innocence in the Garden of Eden; he is thus the arch-thief of all time. It is therefore appropriate that serpents should be the instruments of punishment for thieves. As for the form the punishment takes, we must understand that the thief is more than an economic parasite: Morally, his action is an attack on the integrity of the human personality of his victim. Anyone who has been robbed of a precious possession knows that the shock extends beyond the financial loss incurred. Psychologically, our possessions are an extension of our self; they contribute to our sense of identity. To deprive us of them is to rob us in some measure of that identity. Consequently, the thieves are punished by having their closest possession, the bodies through which they identify themselves and recognize themselves as distinct individuals, taken away from them. No greater loss of identity is possible.

CANTO 26

Moved by the sight of the five Florentine thieves, Dante addresses his native city in bitterly ironic tones: Florence may rejoice in its greatness, since its name spreads even through Hell! The **irony** quickly gives way to deeply felt sorrow and shame for the factious city. The poet prophesies unhappy times for the city and for himself. He and Virgil then move on to the eighth trench, which houses the spirits of evil counselors, who perverted their superior wisdom by using it to deceive others. The very memory of that sorrowful sight, Dante declares, leads him even now to keep tight control over his wit, lest he, too, pervert whatever talent is his by directing it to unvirtuous ends.

The eighth trench gleams with flames like a valley filled with fireflies; each flame contains a soul swathed in the fire that burns it. A single flame with two points holds the souls of Ulysses and Diomed, heroes of *the Iliad*. At Dante's request, Virgil addresses the flame and asks Ulysses to relate the story of his wanderings and his death. Ulysses complies and tells how, after having explored the known world and sailed over the entire Mediterranean, he sailed past the Straits of Gibraltar. He urged his men to explore the world beyond the straits, reminding them that they were not meant to live like brutes, but to follow virtue and knowledge. They came to the Antipodes, within sight of a tall mountain. Their joy at the sight was short-lived, however, for a fierce storm arose and sank the ship.

Comment

Ulysses is placed among the evil counselors for his part in the deceit which brought about the defeat of Troy (Homer already characterizes him as wily and crafty). He is an evil counselor, too, in urging his men to seek a boundless Knowledge, a quest that leads to their destruction. Nonetheless, his passion for knowledge lends him a nobility of spirit which Dante grants to very few of the sinners he meets in Hell. The story of his voyage to the southern hemisphere is completely Dante's invention; the mountain Ulysses and his crew saw is Mount Purgatory.

CANTO 27

The flame of Ulysses leaves; it is followed by another containing the soul of Guido de Montefeltro, a famous Ghibelline warrior who joined the Franciscan order towards the end of his life. He asks if peace reigns in the Romagna (a region in northern Italy), and Dante tells him that though there is no open warfare there, its petty rulers live with strife in their hearts. Guido then tells his story: He had been wily and cunning in war, and thus earned his reputation. Towards the end of his life, he became penitent and confessed his sins, hoping to save his soul. But Pope Boniface VIII, promising him absolution, induced him to sin once more. The pope was at war with the Colonna family, who had retreated to the fortress of Palestrina. Unable to conquer it, the pope asked Guido's advice, and Guido told him to make generous promises but not to keep them. His advice doomed him: Relying on the pope's promise of absolution, he had not repented. Consequently, at his death, a struggle between St. Francis and a devil for his soul ended in the devil's victory.

Comment

There is a tragic note in Count Guido's story. Here is a man who was truly penitent; even Hell has not destroyed his deeply felt concern for the welfare of his people in the Romagna. Yet because of one fatal error - his reliance on the Pope's absolution - he is forever doomed. What lends poignancy to his sorrow is the clear understanding he has of the fact that he alone is ultimately responsible for his fate. He was on the brink of salvation, but St. Francis' charity (i.e., love) could not wash away his sin. His story illustrates the basic Christian fact that no matter how well-intentioned he may be, a man cannot gain salvation if he does not put himself in a state of grace.

CANTO 28

Dante and Virgil now look into the ninth trench, holding the sowers of discord. These sinners are all rent asunder or mutilated, in sign of the mutilations they have inflicted on the spiritual body of the Church, the body politic, and family ties.

The first to come into sight is Mahomet, rent asunder from the chin downwards. His guts hang between his legs, and he pulls his rent chest apart as he exclaims upon his fate. His nephew Ali has his head split open from chin to forehead. Learning that Dante is likely to return to earth, Mahomet sends a warning to Fra Dolcino, whose schismatic doctrines are stirring up strife in northern Italy. Several souls guilty of stirring up political strife now appear, variously mutilated. Finally, the Provencal poet, Bertan de Born, comes by, holding his severed head in his hand as if it were a lantern. He is punished in this way for having set Prince Henry against his father, Henry II of England.

CANTO 29

Dante now looks for the soul of his father's cousin, Geri del Bello; Virgil says that he saw that spirit earlier, shaking an angry fist at Dante. Dante then surmises that Geri is angry because none of his kinsmen have yet avenged his murder.

The poets reach the last section of Malebolge, the tenth ditch, where the counterfeiters are punished. The lamentations coming from there, like arrows barbed with pity, are so piercing that Dante covers his ears with his hands. It is, Dante says, as if all the hospitals of the most unhealthy regions of Tuscany and Sardinia had been emptied into one ditch; the pain and the stench are equally unbearable. Dante then speaks to two alchemists, Griffolino and Capocchio, both covered from head to foot with itchy scabs which they never stop picking at. Griffolino tells Dante that he was put to death for having jokingly told Albero da Siena that he could fly and then having been unable to teach Albero the art. Capocchio, who may have been a friend of Dante's, reminds the poet of his great skill in imitating Nature.

Comment

The falsifiers fall into three classes: 1) those guilty of counterfeiting things - alchemists, forgers, etc.; 2) those guilty of falsifying through deeds - impersonators of others; and 3) those guilty of falsifying through words - liars and false witnesses. Griffolino and Capocchio belong to the first class, as does Master Adam in the next canto; Gianni Schicchi and Myrrha, also in the next canto, belong to the second class; and Sinon and Potiphar's wife to the third.

CANTO 30

Dante next sees two spirits, pale and naked, running around and biting everyone like hungry swine. One is Gianni Schicchi, who had impersonated the dead Buoso Donati and, dictating a false will, left the bulk of Buoso's fortune to himself; he bites Capocchio on the neck-joint and drags him away. The other, Griffolino tells Dante, is Myrrha, who disguised herself as another woman in order to sleep with her father. Those two having gone, Dante turns his attention to Adam of Brescia, who had counterfeited the Florentine gold florin. Swelled with dropsy, he is so heavy that he can scarcely move; he is also tormented by thirst and by the sight of flowing rivers, the water of which he can never taste. Master Adam then identifies two other figures for Dante: They are Potiphar's wife, who falsely accused Joseph of trying to seduce her, and Sinon, the Greek who allowed himself to be captured by the Trojans and persuaded them to bring the wooden horse into the city. Sinon is angered at having his presence disclosed; he starts a brawl with Master Adam, in which they exchange a few blows and a rich collection of insults. Virgil finally takes Dante to task for watching; Dante feels deeply ashamed. Virgil reassures him, telling him he will always be at his side to keep him from the base desire of listening to such quarrels.

INFERNO

. . . .

CANTO 31

The poets now leave the eighth circle, Malebolge. As they move toward the central well, the air is so dark that Dante can hardly see. He seems to discern some towers, but Virgil informs him that they are the upper halves of the bodies of giants who stand around the edge of the central well. They are the Titans who fought against the gods; among them is Nimrod, the reputed builder of the tower of Babel. He is the embodiment of stupidity, and speaks a language all his own which no one understands. The poets then come to Antaeus, who, unlike the other giants, is unfettered because he did not participate in the struggle against the gods. Virgil asks him to lower them into Cocytus, promising that Dante will restore his fame on earth. Antaeus holds out his hand, and the two poets having stepped into it, he sets them down in the ninth and last circle of Hell.

Comment

Nimrod, an example of human pride and arrogance, since he sought to scale the heavens and conquer God, is here revealed as bestially stupid - only abysmal stupidity could lead man to attempt the conquest of God. Since, according to Genesis, it was the tower of Babel that prompted God to give man different languages to replace the one universal language they all spoke, Nimrod is punished by having a language all his own, which no one understands. As he understands no other language, he is effectively isolated, unable to communicate or receive knowledge. He is thus reduced to a state of stupidity which reflects his spiritual ignorance on earth.

CANTO 32

Dante doubts his ability to describe the lowest part of Hell, the bottom of the whole universe; he will proceed cautiously, for the undertaking is not for a child's tongue. He calls on the Muses to sustain him, so that his words may not diverge from the truth.

While Dante is still gazing at the wall, a voice asks him to be careful not to step on anyone's head. He looks down and sees a lake of ice beneath his feet. It is Caina, the first section of Cocytus. Named after Cain, it holds those who were treacherous to their kin. Immersed up to their necks in the ice, they hold their heads downwards while their teeth chatter from the cold. Two of them are so closely pressed together that their hair intertwines; they raise their faces to Dante when he addresses them, and their eyes immediately gush tears which freeze on their lids. Enraged at being so tightly bound together, they butt each other like rams. A third soul, Camicion de' Pazzi, tells Dante that those two are Alessandro and Napoleone degli

Alberti, two brothers who killed each other in a quarrel over their inheritance.

As he moves along, Dante notices that the faces are turned upwards. He is now in Antenora, the second division of Cocytus. It holds those who betrayed their country, and is named after Antenor, the Trojan who, according to a medieval legend, betrayed Troy to the Greeks. Here, whether by will, destiny, or chance, Dante's foot strikes one face, which immediately raises an outcry at such treatment. The soul's reference to the battle of Montaperti leads Dante to ask him his identity. When Dante's request is refused, he threatens to tear the hair off the sinner's head. The latter persists in his refusal, and Dante has already plucked several tufts from the head, when another soul calls the stubborn spirit by name, thus identifying him as Bocca degli Abbati, whose treachery at Montaperti caused the defeat of the Florentine Guelfs. Dante, disgusted, no longer wishes him to speak. But Bocca now names several other sinners punished with him.

Finally, Dante comes upon two spirits frozen in one hole, so close together that one is constantly eating away at the other's head. Stunned by the sight, Dante addresses the eater and asks him to explain the infernal feast, promising to report his story in the world of the living.

CANTO 33

The spirit Dante has spoken to is Ugolino della Gherardesca, leader of one faction of the Guelfs of Pisa; his victim is Ruggieri degli Ubaldi, Archbishop of the city and leader of its Ghibellines. Ugolino had intrigued with Ruggieri to bring about the exile of his grandson, Nino, who led the other Guelf faction; Ruggieri, in turn, betrayed Ugolino and had him imprisoned with his sons and grandsons. It is at this point that Ugolino, wishing to blacken Ruggieri's reputation, picks up the story. One day, as he and his children were waiting for their food, they heard the entrance to the tower being locked; from that moment on they were left to starve. On the second day, seeing the expression on his sons' faces, he bit his hands out of despair; the children, thinking him hungry, offered themselves as food. On the fourth day, his son Gaddo fell at his feet, crying for help; there he died. The other three fell one by one between the fifth and sixth days, leaving him alone to mourn over the dead bodies. Finally, as he puts it, hunger was more powerful than grief.

Having finished his tale, Ugolino once again seizes Ruggieri's skull and begins to gnaw at it. Dante, horrified by what he has heard, breaks out into an invective against Pisa, which he calls the shame of Italy. Even if Ugolino was guilty of betrayal, his sons were innocent and did not deserve their torture.

Dante and Virgil move further on. They come to a section where the spirits are lying on their backs on the frozen lake; as their tears freeze on their eyelids, they have no outlet for their grief. Instead, it turns inward and increases their agony. They are in Ptolemea (named after the Ptolemy of 1 Maccabees who treacherously killed his guests), the third section of Cocytus, where those who betrayed their friends and guests are punished. In this region Dante is surprised to feel a movement of air. Since all heat is absent here, there should be no motion. When he asks Virgil what causes the wind, he is told that he will soon see for himself. In the meantime one of the souls frozen to the lake asks him to remove the ice from its eyes. Dante agrees, on condition that the speaker identify himself, adding the wish that he may go to the bottom of the ice if he does not help the suffering soul. The speaker then reveals himself as Fra Alberigo, the one who had invited his brother and nephew to a feast and had them killed. Dante is surprised to learn that he is dead, but Alberigo explains that it often happens that a treacherous soul falls to Ptolemea before the death of the body. The body is kept alive by a demon who takes the place of the soul. Alberigo then refers to another spirit, lying behind him; it is the Genoese Branca d'Oria, and Dante must know, having just come from the world of the living, if his body is still alive. Lastly, he asks Dante to open his eyes for him. But Dante refuses, explaining that to be rude to such a sinner was a courtesy. The canto closes with a brief invective against Genoa, a city which produces such vile souls that one of them has sunk to Hell before its appointed time.

Comment

Dante's wish that he may go to the bottom of the ice if he does not help Alberigo may seem surprising, but it is easily explained. Dante knows full well that he is going to the bottom of Hell, since that is the only way for him to leave the place; he merely takes advantages of his knowledge to get Alberigo's story. His subsequent refusal to keep his word may appear crude and uncalled for, but we must remember that Dante is now so deep in Hell that there is very little call on our sympathy for the sinners he finds there. Ptolemea is but one step removed from the heart of evil, Judecca.

CANTO 34

Virgil and Dante now reach the last section of Cocytus, Judecca, so named after Judas Iscariot, and reserved for the punishment of traitors to their lords and benefactors. Satan is at the center, and Virgil urges Dante to look for him. But first Dante observes how the other sinners are punished; they are completely immersed in the frozen lake, some lying, some standing upright or on their heads, some doubled-up. The icy blasts of wind are so strong that Dante must take shelter behind Virgil. But when they reach a point from which Satan is visible, Virgil moves aside and makes Dante stop and look at him. "I did not die," says Dante, "and did not remain alive."

Feeling as if he had been deprived of both life and death, Dante stares at the "emperor of the dolorous realm," who stands at the center of the frozen lake, rising from the waist above the surface of the lake. Observing him, Dante muses that if he was once as beautiful as he is ugly now, and still raised his eyes against his Maker, he can indeed be the source of all human woe. He has three faces, the middle one crimson, the one on the right white and yellow, and the one on the left black. Under each face rises a pair of wings shaped like those of a bat. These wings are in constant motion as he tries to extricate himself from the ice; yet it is their motion which produces the icy winds which keep Cocytus frozen and keep him imprisoned. With each mouth he chews on a sinner; in the center he holds Judas, while the two sides hold Brutus and Cassius.

Having seen all there is to see, Dante clasps Virgil's neck, and the two poets begin the fearful descent along the shaggy side of Satan. When they reach the hip, Virgil turns himself upside down and pulls himself up by Satan's hair, so that Dante thinks they are returning to Hell again. Virgil pulls himself through an opening in the rock, and sets Dante down; now Dante sees the legs of Satan turned upwards. His guide explains that they have passed the center of the earth, and must now climb up to the surface of the southern hemisphere. When Lucifer - i.e., Satan - fell, Virgil continues, all the land where the devil struck the earth moved northward, and the sea covered the area. However, he adds, the ground at the core of the earth may have rushed upwards to form Mount Purgatory, which is their immediate goal.

There is a passage, Dante then tells us, formed by a stream which ate its way through the rock down to the cavern below Cocytus. It is this road that Virgil now takes, and the two poets climb untiringly, Virgil first and Dante behind him. At last Dante catches sight of the beauties of heaven through a round opening; emerging to the surface, he can now once more see the stars.

Comment

The three sinners mawed by Satan's three mouths are the arch-traitors of mankind, who betrayed the spiritual and political order of the world. Judas Iscariot betrayed Christ; Brutus and Cassius murdered Julius Caesar; between them, they attacked the spiritual and temporal principles designed to rule mankind.

The stream which flows towards Hell is Lethe, the river of forgetfulness of classical mythology, which finds its source in the Garden of Eden atop Mount Purgatory. There the sins of the purged souls are washed away. The river then carries these sins back to Hell, where they belong. Since Hell is the source of all sin, it is only right that all sins should be returned there.

Dante's picture of the heart of Hell departs from popular tradition, which would see it as a place of fire and brimstone presided over by a malicious and clever devil. Instead, Dante demonstrates once again the inherent stupidity of evil: All that Lucifer has accomplished by his rebellion against God is to render himself impotent.

Far from being the active, clever devil whom we secretly admire, he is completely passive, totally incapacitated as he stands forever frozen in the lake which is of his own making. The only motion he is capable of is the mechanical flapping of his bat-like wings and the champing of his three mouths; the wings set in motion the chilly winds of evil, but it is these winds which keep the lake frozen and Lucifer imprisoned. Evil is not only stupid, but self-destructive as well.

Evil is nonetheless a temptation which must be recognized and faced if it is to be overcome. Dante must therefore view Lucifer squarely in his total ugliness. Once he has had this total experience of evil, reason can move him beyond the paralyzed stage in which he feels neither dead nor alive.

Dante feels neither dead nor alive when face to face with Lucifer because Lucifer is the absolute death of the spirit. He is the dead center of the universe, the antithesis of God, who is the source, principle, and highest incarnation of life. His three faces are thus a travesty of the Holy Trinity against which he rebelled. To the Middle Ages, the Father, Son, and Holy Ghost represented the unity of divine power, wisdom, and love; Satan's three faces represent their opposites. Thus his crimson face represents his hatred; his white and yellow face, his impotence; and his black face, his ignorance. These are all negative attributes. When man gives himself to sin, he puts himself in their power and moves toward spiritual death.

Finally, the devil is ugly. He stands at the opposite pole of the beauty which draws man towards heaven. Only after Dante has taken in the full force of that ugliness, only after he has really seen the full ugliness of sin, can he begin to rise, under the guidance of reason. As he emerges from the bowels of the earth, the sight of the stars shining in the heavens assures him that he is moving towards his goal. After his journey through the realm of darkness, their light restores him to life. It also holds out the promise of the fuller life to be found in heaven. The stars, with which each of the three sections of *the Divine Comedy* concludes, stand as a symbol of Dante's highest aspiration. They also stand as a symbol of the divine order. It is therefore fitting that they should come into view as Dante rises from the center of the earth. There is relevance, too, in the fact that he began his journey on Good Friday and emerges from Hell on the day of Resurrection, Easter Sunday. Henceforth, these stars are going to be the signpost by which he will guide himself.

PURGATORIO

. . . .

The physical structure of Dante's Purgatory is simpler than that of Hell. Mount Purgatory is a conically shaped mountain rising in the midst of the sea which covers the southern hemisphere. It consists of three sections. Antepurgatory holds the souls of the excommunicate and the late-repentant, who must wait a given number of years before they can begin the purgation of their souls. Purgatory proper consists of a series of seven terraces where the seven deadly sins are purged. Each terrace is reached by climbing a staircase guarded by an angel; each terrace also presents examples (by inscription or by voice) of the virtue corresponding to the sin that is being expurgated, as well as examples of famous persons guilty of that sin. The Garden of Eden, finally, is the seat of earthly perfection.

According to Virgil (*Inferno*, 34) the mountain was thrown up when Satan was hurled down to the center of the earth. In other words, the fall of the angels caused a part of the earth to leap heavenward; this leap made it worthy to receive man, who was then created to replace the angels lost to the love of God. When man fell, however, he lost not only the perfect heavenly life (which was going to be revealed to him), but the perfect earthly life as well. No longer perfect, he was expelled from the Garden of Eden. His first task, before he can get to heaven, is therefore to recover the Garden of Eden - i.e., recover the earthly perfection he has lost. He must, hence, be cleansed of his sins, and the mountain is the scene of that purgation.

Since the immediate goal of Purgatorio is the Garden of Eden, the recovery of earthly perfection, it is primarily concerned with ethical, rather than spiritual, truth. Purgatorio has neither the drama of Inferno, nor the dazzling spiritual intensity of Paradiso; its particular beauty lies in the thoroughgoing exploration of moral philosophy under the guidance of human reason. Its methodical development of a livable human ethics comes to fruition in the earthly paradise. There the moral idealism of the poem culminates in the allegorical pageant of the true relation of Church and State; it shines in the eyes of Beatrice, in the flashing light of which Dante can read the double nature of Christ; and it finds its justification in the final purgation of Dante's soul.

PURGATORIO

TEXTUAL ANALYSIS

CANTOS 1-4

....

| CANTO 1

Dante declares that he will sing of the second realm, where the soul is cleansed of sin and made worthy to ascend to heaven. First he expresses the delight he experienced at the sight of the pure sky in the rising dawn. He sees Venus in the eastern horizon; then, turning towards the south pole, he sees a constellation of four stars never seen by man since the Fall banished him to the northern hemisphere. So glorious is their light that the heavens rejoice at it, Dante declares, and he bemoans the fact that the "northern clime" can never behold them.

Turning north, Dante sees a venerable old man in whose face shine the rays of the four stars. It is Cato, the guardian of Mount Purgatory, who takes Dante and Virgil to task because he thinks they are damned souls who have somehow escaped from Hell. Virgil explains who they are and asks Cato to help them on their journey. In the name of the heavenly lady who sent Virgil to Dante, Cato agrees; he orders Virgil to wash the hue of Hell from

Dante's face with dew, and to gird him with a rush plucked from the shore. He then tells them to find their way by following the rising sun. The two poets follow his instructions; Dante's face is washed, and as Virgil plucks a rush from the ground, another immediately springs up to take its place.

Comment

Dante's delight in the physical beauty of the world stands in sharp contrast to his despair at the beginning of Inferno. No longer lost, he feels restored to the mainstream of life. The planet Venus is the third heaven, the heaven of Love; its appearance over the horizon is a token of the divine love which draws him on. The four stars indicate the nature of the realm he has just entered. They symbolize the four cardinal or moral virtues, Prudence, Justice, Fortitude, and Temperance. These are the virtues of the active life, the virtues which regulate the moral life of man and of society. They are not exclusively Christian; they are reflected in the face of Cato, the ancient Roman who himself symbolizes virtue, and who is therefore the appointed guardian of Purgatory. Cato's stern aspect is further indication of the moral discipline required for the ascent of Mount Purgatory; his moral integrity, which takes its direction from heaven (the four stars), is a necessary addition to human reason, which alone cannot find its way (Virgil asks Cato to direct them).

At this early stage Dante still has to find the way of penitence, and although Cato orders the washing of Dante's face, he does not tell the poets the way. Cleansed of the contamination of sin and girt with humility (the rush), Dante must find his own way to the life of penitence, still relying on the help of reason. The only hint Cato can give the two poets is that they are to follow the path of the sun, i.e., God.

It becomes clear that whereas in *Inferno* Dante was primarily an observer, although at times profoundly involved in what he observed, in Purgatorio he becomes an active participant in the process of purgation. No longer an observer, he is an actor on whose brow will be inscribed the seven P's representing the seven deadly sins (Canto 9). These will be wiped away only as he moves through the seven terraces of purgation; then he will be ready to be received in the earthly paradise.

CANTO 2

The sun is setting in Jerusalem, Dante tells us, as it dawns at Mount Purgatory. He and Virgil stand on the shore, pondering on their course, when they see a bright light approaching. It is an angel, ferrying the soul of the saved to Purgatory. As they alight, the souls sing the Psalm "When Israel went out of Egypt." The angel makes the sign of the cross and departs. The sun now fully lights the sky, and the new arrivals ask Virgil and Dante the way. Virgil answers that they, too, are strangers; the spirits then notice Dante's breath in the air, and realize that he is still alive in the "first life."

Eagerly curious, they throng around him; one, especially, gazes at him with intense affection. It is the musician Casella, a good friend of Dante's, and three times Dante tries to embrace him and clasps nothing but his own breast. Realizing that an empty shade is not to be embraced, he briefly explains his presence in Purgatory; Casella, in turn, explains the delay between the time of his death and his soul's arrival there. First, Casella declares, the justice of God's will is not to be questioned: Whatever the reason for the angel's refusal to pick him up at the mouth of the Tiber, where he was waiting, it is justified. But, he continues, for the past three months he has been picking up all who would be ferried to the mountain. Dante then asks him, if the power of music survives the change of death, to calm his soul as he was wont by singing the song "Love that discourseth to me in my mind." Casella begins singing and holds everyone's rapt attention. But the stern Cato suddenly appears and rebukes the souls for their negligent tarrying; they immediately hurry across the plain towards the mountain, leaving Dante and Virgil alone once more.

Comment

The notation of the change from day to night and back in Purgatorio is significant. First, it marks the return to "normal" life after the harrowing journey through Hell. As the poets learn afterwards, no one can move forward in Purgatory at night: Only during the day can they climb; at night they must rest. Second, the alternation between daylight and darkness underscores Purgatory's position between Hell, where total darkness reigns, and Paradise, which is pure light. The middle position of the earth - and therefore of man - is thus emphasized. The concern with the sun's movement across the sky is consequently more than just a piece of astronomical pedantry: It is yet one more reminder of that fact that *Purgatorio* deals with man's earthly journey. It is this fact which accounts for the marked ethical tone of this second section of Dante's poem.

In a letter to his patron and protector, Can Grande della Scala, lord of Verona, Dante gave a mystical interpretation of the opening line of the psalm sung by the souls arriving in Purgatory. On the mystical (or "anagogical," as he called it) level, the words "When Israel went out of Egypt" signified "the departure of the sanctified sold from the slavery of this corruption to the liberty of eternal glory." The psalm was part of the Church's last rites for the dying and burial of the dead.

The souls of the saved gather at the mouth of the Tiber, the river of Rome, just as those of the damned sink to the banks of Acheron in Hell. In other words, salvation is to be attained only in the true Church, which has its seat in Rome. The importance Dante attaches to the Church, and therefore to the Papacy, is indicated by the fact that Casella was finally ferried to Purgatory: His mention of the "past three months" is a reference to the plenary indulgence granted by the pope to all pilgrims during the Jubilee year 1300. The fact that the pope is none other than the hated Boniface VIII (see *Inferno*, Cantos 19 and 27) does not make his acts spiritually less effective or authoritative.

The song of love Casella sings is an early poem of Dante's, which was interpreted by Dante in the Convivio as praising Lady Philosophy. An echo of Dante's intense interest in scholastic speculation, it holds not only his attention, but that of Virgil and the other souls as well. Even reason can forget its function, and Cato has to appear to recall the souls to their business, which is the active participation in salvation by climbing the mountain. To listen to a song, to follow the speculations of philosophy - these alone will not bring the soul to God. The moral business of life calls for training in virtue, as Cato sternly reminds the souls. That this episode at the beginning of Dante's journey through Purgatory represents an important lesson for the education of the soul is manifest by the way in which Beatrice receives Dante in the earthly paradise. There, at the end of this part of his spiritual pilgrimage, she reproves him severely for that very dedication to philosophy - the subject of Casella's song - which caused him to lose his way (Canto 30).

CANTO 3

After the flight of the newly arrived souls, Dante feels confused and Virgil remorseful. Yet Dante draws close to his companion, for, he asks, who can bring him up the mountain if not Virgil? Both now turn towards the mountain, and, with the sun behind them, Dante is momentarily frightened by the absence of Virgil's shadow next to his. He thinks Virgil has abandoned him, but he is reassured as his companion reminds him that his body is buried in Naples. If the form he wears casts no shadow, he should be no more amazed than at the fact that the heavenly spheres do not prevent light from passing through them. Reason cannot fathom the mystery of God's ways; if it could, Virgil adds, there would have been no need of redemption, and men like Plato and Aristotle would not now be yearning with hopeless desire in Limbo.

The poets now reach the base of the mountain which is so steep that no ascent is possible. As Virgil pauses, trying to find a way up, Dante notices a group of spirits coming from the left, but so slowly that they hardly seem to move. He suggests to Virgil that they go towards them to get the information they seek. Coming near them the souls gaze in amazement at Dante's shadow. Virgil quickly explains why Dante has a shadow. The souls, in answer to Virgil's request for direction, tell the two poets to reverse their course. One of them, King Manfred, tells the story of his death at the battle of Benevento, and the shameful treatment accorded his body by order of the Pope. It is from Manfred's story that Dante learns that these are the excommunicate; from Manfred, too, he learns that the effects of the Church's malediction are limited. If the excommunicate repents, Manfred tells Dante, he need not lose hope of redemption; he must, however, wait thirty times the duration of his excommunication before he can begin the purgation of his sins in Purgatory. Prayer by the living, he adds, can shorten this period.

Comment

Dante's shadow and the absence of Virgil's indicate the dualism of body and soul which is the central proposition of Christian doctrine and central to man's experience in life. The flesh imposes its limitations on the soul; it obstructs the sun's rays and its vision of reality is consequently limited. Only experience, the experience garnered in Purgatory, will resolve this dualism.

Reason's own limitations are further illustrated by Virgil's explicit statement to that effect and his inability to find the way up the mountain by himself. All during the journey through Purgatory, Virgil is far less sure of himself than he was in the journey through Hell; more than once he and Dante will be enlightened by some soul they meet on the way. Here reason's wisdom consists in knowing it must look beyond itself for the guidance of the soul on the road to penitence. But Virgil is not only reason; he also represents the Empire, the ordered moral and social life of mankind. That is why Dante clings all the closer to him, even at the very moment when he acknowledges his shortcomings. For without the social and moral order regulating the life of man, Dante could never find the path to salvation. As in *Inferno*, the vision in *Purgatorio* has reference to man's experience; specifically it is man's experience in a socially and morally structured world that is being staged.

CANTO 4

Dante's attention has been so much absorbed by Manfred's speech that he has not noticed the passing of time. The fact, he says, refutes the Platonic doctrine of the plurality of souls; for, he says, if each of our faculties had a separate soul, the absorption of one would not impair the functioning of another.

The excommunicate then point the passage through which Virgil and Dante must climb to reach the slope of the mountain; it is a narrow cleft in the rock, which must be climbed, not only with hands and feet, but with the "swift wings of great desire." Finally, they reach an embankment and pause to rest. Dante is surprised to see the sun on his left, even though he is facing east, and Virgil reminds him that they are now in the southern hemisphere. Then Dante wishes to know how high the mountain is, since he cannot see its top. Virgil merely tells him that it is such that the higher one gets, the easier the climb becomes. When the climbing becomes so easy that he feels like a boat running down stream, then he may hope to rest.

This discourse is interrupted by a voice from behind a huge boulder, which declares ironically that Dante will probably experience a keen desire for rest before he gets that high. Moving towards the boulder, the poets discover the souls of the late-repentant; among them is the speaker, Belacqua, a Florentine friend of Dante's. Having postponed repentance for his sins until his death, he is excluded from purgation for as many years as he lived impenitent on earth. Only the prayers of some soul in grace can shorten the waiting period. The poets then proceed on their journey.

PURGATORIO

....

CANTO 5

Dante's shadow continues to amaze the souls he and Virgil pass, but Virgil reproves Dante for delaying and paying heed to their exclamations. A group singing the Miserere break into exclamations of wonder at the sight of Dante's shadow; the poets stop to speak with its members. They are the souls of those who suffered a violent death and repented at the very last moment. They all come forward to ask for prayers from the living, and Virgil will let Dante listen to them provided that he keeps walking. Jacopo del Cassero describes how he was assassinated at the orders of Azzo VIII of Este. Then Buonconte da Montefeltro, son of Guido da Montefeltro (see *Inferno*, Canto 28), steps forward. Dante asks him why his body was never found after the battle of Campaldino (1289). He explains that he died, mortally wounded on the bank of the Archiano, where it flows into the Arno. He died calling on the Virgin Mary, and an angel of God took his soul. A devil who had hoped to snatch his soul became so angry that he took his revenge on the body, which he caused to be tossed into the river by a storm. Lastly, a lady of Siena, Pia, identifies herself and asked to be remembered by Dante. (She was apparently murdered by her husband.) Siena, she says, bored her; Maremma undid her. The facts of her life are well known to the man who betrothed and married her with his ring.

Comment

The mysterious moment of death is in the forefront of this canto. The violently slain, unprepared for death and facing it without priestly ministrations, are nonetheless granted the last illumination which saves them. Buonconte's story thus contrasts sharply with that of his father, who, for all his caution and repentance, lost eternal salvation; Pia's story, all the more touching for its cryptic brevity, contrasts similarly with that of Francesca, another woman violently slain by her husband (*Inferno*, Canto 5).

CANTO 6

The souls of the late-repentant who died by violence throng about Dante, asking to be remembered in their families' prayers. Dante then asks Virgil to explain how it is that these souls are so anxious for prayers, when he, Virgil, had expressly declared that the Fates could not be bent by prayer. Virgil answers that there is no contradiction. First, he says, the Divine Will is not actually bent by prayer: If the necessary atonement is offered by the love of those left behind, then divine justice is satisfied. Besides, Virgil adds, his statement (*Aeneid*, vi, 376) is not relevant here since the prayers he spoke of were those of heathens, severed from God. Finally, he tells Dante, Beatrice will resolve any further doubts on this question.

Hearing the name of Beatrice, Dante is eager to proceed, hoping to reach the summit by the end of the day. But Virgil tells him that it will be several days before he reaches that goal. The sun having moved further across the sky, the poets are now in the shade of the mountain, and Dante casts no shadow. They perceive the soul of Sordello gazing upon them like a crouching lion. Virgil asks him the way, but he disdains to answer. When, however, Virgil tells him he is from Mantua, Sordello leaps up and embraces his fellow citizen. The sight of Sordello's joy leads Dante to inveigh against Italy, so divided against itself that it refuses to accept the central authority that should apply universal Roman law. He accuses the emperors, Rudolf I and Albert I, of abandoning Italy to disorder. But Florence is sarcastically excepted from this diatribe - its haughtiness, its perversion of justice, its constant changes in law, customs, etc., are excoriated in a bitterly ironic attack.

Comment

In *the Aeneid* Aeneas' steersman, Palinurus, was drowned and was refused admittance to the underworld because his body was unburied. He was told by the Sybil to stop hoping that the decrees of the gods could be bent by his prayers. It is this passage Dante has in mind when he takes up the question of the real force of intercession by his prayers. On the positive side, Virgil tells him that intercession is the fire of love which can in a moment fulfill the work of years in the soul. Prayer here is grace in action, fulfilling the requirements of divine justice for another soul, and establishing a community between souls. In this way prayer is not really "bending" the divine will; it acts in accordance with that will. On the negative side, Palinurus' prayer was ineffectual because as a pagan he was excluded from divine grace. Finally, the whole question is referred to Beatrice because it is a mystery of grace which reason cannot solve.

Sordello was an Italian poet, a late troubadour who wrote in Provencal. His role as guide of the poets to the Valley of Negligent Rulers (see next canto) is due to his famous lament for a Provencal baron. In that poem Sordello advised the chief rulers of Europe to eat his hero's heart in order to gain his nobility and courage.

CANTO 7

After embracing Virgil several times, Sordello asks his name. On learning who he is, Sordello falls at his feet and embraces his knees. Virgil then tells him of his abode in Limbo, and of the state of the souls there, where the lamentations are as sighs on the part of those who practiced the cardinal virtues but did not know the three holy theological virtues. Virgil then asks Sordello for the way to Purgatory proper, and Sordello offers to guide them. But, Sordello adds, it is impossible to ascend at night, and since day is falling, they should look for some resting place. The news surprises Virgil, who wants to know whether one cannot of one's own will climb after dark, or whether others would prevent one's ascent. Sordello then draws a line on the ground and tells Virgil that he could not step over it after sunset, and that it is the darkness of night that would hamper the will with lack of power. After nightfall, one can only go down, not up.

Sordello then leads Virgil and Dante to a valley in which are found the souls of kings and rulers who had neglected the true function of their office for the selfish pleasure of their comfort or the equally selfish pleasure of waging war. The valley in which they sit is truly beautiful, but the relief from the serious cares of life it affords them is no comfort to them; it is a source of anguish which makes them yearn all the more for the active purgation to be found higher up on the mountain. As the poets approach, the rulers are singing the hymn Salva Regina ("Hail, Queen," sung at Vespers, the last service of the day). Sordello points out various rulers. Some, old enemies, sing in harmony and comfort one another; others bewail the sins of their still living sons.

Comment

The striking feature of this canto is Virgil's total dependence on Sordello. Although he is the greater poet by far (a fact acknowledged by Sordello's falling at his feet), Virgil is at a disadvantage when it comes to knowledge relating to the purgation and redemption of the soul. It is from Sordello that he learns the law of ascent on Mount Purgatory: As long as the sun, symbol of the radiance of God, shines, the soul may rise; at night, in the dark, it must patiently wait for the renewal of day. The contrast between Christian and pagan experience is clearly marked: To follow the cardinal or moral virtues is not enough, and ignorance of the three theological virtues excludes one from salvation. This much is made clear by Virgil's position in Limbo. It is underlined by the further contrast between the hopelessness of the residents of Limbo with the hopeful waiting of the negligent rulers in their valley. The wait may be painful, but there is an end in sight, and they can pray to the Virgin Mary to intercede for them with her Son.

CANTO 8

The souls in the valley round out the day by singing their evening hymn, Te lucis ante ("Before the ending of the day"), and then gaze upward expectantly. Two angels descend and take up guard with blunted swords. Clad in green, they come from Mary's bosom, Sordello explains, and guard the valley against the night visitation of a serpent. Sordello and his companions then descend into the valley, where Dante encounters an acquaintance, Nino de' Visconti, who is shocked, as is Sordello, to learn that Dante is still alive. Nino then asks Dante to have his daughter pray for him, since his wife, having remarried, has forgotten him. Dante then gazes heavenward, and instead of the four stars he saw in the morning, he sees three stars flaming in the sky like torches. At this moment the serpent - "perchance such as gave the bitter food to Eve" - appears, making its way through the grass and flowers. It is put to flight by the noise of the guardian angels' green wings.

Nino had called Conrad Malaspina to come witness the miracle of God's grace, which permitted Dante to travel through Hell and Purgatory while still in the "first life." He asks for news of his land, and Dante replies that although he has never been in his dominions, his house has an illustrious reputation throughout the world: His successors are noted for their virtue and nobility. In return, Conrad predicts that before seven years have passed Dante will personally experience his family's courtesy and will have occasion to fix that opinion of them all the more firmly in his mind.

Comment

The hymn Te lucis ante was a prayer which asked God to protect man against dreams and phantoms of the night, and to restrain man's enemy. Clearly, it is to the temptations of the night, when the moral will is least active, that the **episode** of the serpent has reference. Evil is still a mystery unfathomable by man's rational faculty. There are hidden regions of the soul - we would say the subconscious - which are not subject to the moral will. Against the temptations which beset such regions, one must put one's hope in God (the green wings of the angels signify hope). What is equally significant is that the four stars representing the moral virtues have vanished and have been replaced by the three representing the theological virtues. The lesson is clear: The moral will alone cannot overcome evil; to do so one must be armed with divine grace (the three stars, the angels who come from the bosom of Mary). Such is the lesson Dante wishes to teach on the threshold of Purgatory.

To reach the theological virtues, one must develop sound moral will. The fact that one can ascend only during the day, when the four stars symbolizing those virtues are above the horizon, indicates that the proper business of Purgatory is ethical. And ethical value has nothing to do with political partisanship: Nino Visconti, a Guelph, and Conrad Malaspina, a Ghibelline, receive equal treatment at Dante's hands. Furthermore, it is the Ghibelline Malaspinas who will receive the exiled Florentine poet, a Guelph, and extend him their hospitality.

CANTO 9

Dante, exhausted by his hitherto sleepless journey, falls into a deep sleep. Towards morning, when dreams are almost prophetic, he dreams he sees a golden eagle poised in the sky, ready to swoop. It also seems to him that he is in the very region from which Ganymede was rapt to heaven. Suddenly the eagle swoops down and lifts him to the region of fire where they both burn. The sensation of burning is so strong that it awakens him; he now finds himself alone with Virgil, higher on the mountain, close to the gate of Purgatory. Virgil informs him that St. Lucy carried him there while he slept.

Dante now follows his guide to the three steps which lead to the gate. The gate is guarded by an angel armed with a sword and clothed in grey, who challenges the newcomers. Virgil replies that a heavenly lady brought them hither, and the angel bids them approach. The first step is of smooth white marble, so polished that Dante can see himself in it; the second, of a rough, dark, calcinated stone, broken by fissures; the third, of flaming red porphyry. The threshold itself, on which the angel sits, is made of adamant. Dante begs the angel to unlock the door. The angel, having carved seven P's on Dante's brow, turns the gold and silver keys and admits Dante into Purgatory. The gate squeaks on its hinge, and Dante's ears catch the sound of a Te Deum being sung.

Comment

Dante's dream of the eagle is symbolic of baptismal regeneration. According to the medieval "Bestiaries," the eagle in his old age flies to the circle of fire, where he burns off all his feathers, and falls into a fountain of water. But here the symbolism is attached to the notion of Empire since the eagle is also symbolic of the Empire, and since Ganymede, who was rapt to heaven by the bird of Jupiter (the eagle), was the son of Tros, and ancestor of Aeneas. The dream, a **foreshadowing** of Dante's purification, is also a vision of the ethical **theme** of *Purgatorio*: the moral and social ordering of life so as to lead to earthly perfection. (It is, after all, while asleep in the valley of the negligent rulers that Dante has this dream). But again, the fusion of personal experience with public import is remarkable, since the dream also reflects the experience of the sleeping Dante as he is being carried upwards to the gate of Purgatory by St. Lucy, illuminating grace, who can bestow such visions, and whom reason must be content to follow.

The angel at the gate represents the ideal priesthood; clothed in the color of ashes, he, too, symbolizes penitence. The sword represents divine justice, reflecting the sun's rays - i.e., the light of God - so that it blinds the sinner. The three steps represent the three parts of the sacrament of Penance - contrition of the heart, confession by the lips, and satisfaction by works. Thus the first, in which Dante can see himself, represents his self-knowledge and the sincerity of his contrition; the second, of dark broken stone, expresses the anguish of the broken heart confessing; the third, the color of love, symbolizes his desire to give satisfaction, to make amends for his sins through love. The adamant threshold on which the angel sits represents the authority of the Church, by which it holds the keys to the kingdom of heaven: "Thou art Peter, and upon this rock I will build my church, ... and I will give unto thee the keys of the kingdom of heaven" (Matthew, xvi, 18–19). The seven P's indicate the seven deadly sins (P stands for peccato, the Italian for sin). These are carved into Dante's flesh and must be purged away on the seven terraces of Purgatory. The symbolism here is an elaborate depiction of the nature of penitence, but penitence only begins at the gate.

CANTO 10

The poets climb a narrow cleft in the rock to reach the first terrace of Purgatory. It stretches in either direction as far as the eye can see; in width it approximates the height of three human bodies. On the inner side are carved scenes from sacred and pagan history, illustrating humility, and Dante comments on their beauty and their truth to life which, he says, would put Nature to shame. First is a depiction of the Annunciation, in which the Virgin Mary's humble attitude seems to bespeak the words "Behold the handmaiden of God." Then Dante sees a scene representing the return of the ark of the covenant, with King David dancing and singing before it. Finally, Dante looks at a carving of the Roman emperor Trajan, whose worth, according to a medieval legend, moved St. Gregory to pray for his return to earth (from Limbo) so that he might embrace Christianity and attain salvation. Virgil then calls Dante's attention to the proud, approaching slowly, bent over and stooping low under the burden of heavy stones they are carrying. This is their punishment for having exalted themselves, mere worms, beyond reason during their life on earth. Their pride is now brought low, and they bewail the fact that they can bear no heavier burden.

PURGATORIO

CANTO 11–15

. . . .

CANTO 11

The souls doing penance for their pride approach, reciting a paraphrase of the Lord's Prayer, the prayer being uttered for the sake of those they have left behind. Once again, Virgil asks the way, and one of the souls directs the poets to turn to the right and circle the mount with the sun. It is the Sienese Omberto Aldobrandesco, whose pride in his ancestry made him so insolvent as to involve himself and his family in ruin. Dante, having bent down in order to listen to Omberto's story, keeps walking with the once proud in this bent position, when another soul twists his head from beneath his load and calls to Dante. Dante recognizes him as the miniature painter and illuminator, Oderisi, who is now willing to admit the greater beauty of a rival's work. Oderisi delivers himself of a brief homily on the fickleness of fame, which barely outlives a generation; he illustrates it with reference to the painter Cimabue, whose reputation has now been eclipsed by his successor Giotto. Similarly, says Oderisi, in poetry, one Guido has supplanted the other, and a third may yet supplant them both. To illustrate his point further, Oderisi points to a third soul, Provenzan Salvani, who sought to take all Siena in his power. Only because he once humiliated himself for the sake of a friend, begging in the streets of Siena for his ransom, has he been allowed into Purgatory instead of being made to wait in Antepurgatory.

CANTO 12

Dante has been walking bent over while listening to Oderisi, and now Virgil bids him to walk faster. He therefore straightens himself, but is still, he says, bowed down in heart. Virgil then calls his attention to the pavement on which are carved numerous examples of the proud fallen low, beginning with Lucifer, the fallen angel, and ending with a picture of Troy in ashes and ruins. Again Dante comments on the amazing life-like quality of the work. At last the poets reach the angel of humility who, with a stroke of his wings, erases the first P on Dante's brow. As Dante and Virgil are about to mount the steps leading to the next terrace, the first Beatitude, "Blessed be the poor in spirit," reaches their ears. Ascending the stairs, Dante marvels at the fact that it seems so much easier going than his journey on the flat terrace; Virgil then informs him that the first P has been erased, and that the others have consequently faded as well. When, Virgil adds, all the P's shall have been removed, then the ascent will not only seem easy, but Dante's feet will move upward with pleasure. Dante checks his forehead with his fingers and finds, indeed, that only six P's are left.

Comment

The pattern of purgation of sin revealed on the first terrace of Purgatory is identical with what occurs on the other terraces.

Purgatory is, as it were, an ordered, disciplined school for souls. The first sight that greets the penitents are examples of humility; in other words, the first step of corrective penance is an awareness of the grace opposite to the sin being purged. With the memory of how God exalts the humble in their minds, the proud are then bent low; only then are they shown how God casts down the proud.

Pride is the most serious sin; before Dante can move up, it must be erased. Not only must it be erased, but when it is, the mark made by the other sins is noticeably lightened, as Dante discovers when he feels his brow. To be delivered from pride makes the healing of the other sins a much easier task, and therefore the climb becomes less difficult.

Dante's conversation with Oderisi is interesting because it reveals his knowledge of and keen interest in the pictorial art of his time. He is aware of the difference between the French art of illuminated manuscripts and the fresco painting on church walls practiced in Italy by Cimabue and his pupil Giotto. Possessed with a keen visual imagination, Dante sees art as a form of truth which is sometimes truer than what is found in Nature.

Dante the author also introduces an ironic note directed at himself in Oderisi's discourse. When Oderisi relates the evolution in painting to that in poetry, he not only refers to the supplanting of one Guido by another, but suggests that a third may yet arise who will replace both. The reference to the two Guidos had been variously interpreted. One Guido may be Guido Guinizelli, founder of the idealistic school of lyric poetry known as the "sweet new style" or "stilnovism." The other maybe Dante's friend, like Dante a follower of Guinizelli, Guido Cavalcanti. It has also been suggested that Oderisi has in mind Guittone d'Arezzo, representative of a non-idealistic tradition, and Guido Guinizelli.

But whoever the two Guidos may be, it is generally agreed that that third poet is none other than Dante himself. This hint of his own outstanding excellence, thrown out in the very place where pride is purged, is followed by a strong statement of the utter vanity of earthly fame. It is characteristic of Dante so to express, and at the same time rebuke, his own pride.

CANTO 13

The second terrace is of dark rock, seemingly deserted, without marks of any kind by which the poets may guide themselves. Virgil addresses the sun and decides to follow it in its path from east to west. Then voices are heard, singing out in praise of kindness and generosity; they sing of Mary's consideration for a neighbor at the marriage in Cana (John ii:3), of the friendship of Orestes and Pylades, and of Christ's command that men love their enemies. Virgil anticipates the fact that examples of envy will reach their ears before the second P is erased from Dante's brow.

The once envious spirits now appear, calling on the love of Mary, of the angels, and of the saints. They who once looked upon the world with envy do penance by having their eyes shut to the beauties of the world: The lids are drawn together with a suture of wire such as is used to tame wild hawks. They now lean on one another, totally dependent on one another for love and support. Looking at them with their sightless eyes, Dante feels guilty, as though he were taking advantage of them, and with Virgil's permission, addresses them. He asks whether there be any Italians among them; he is told that they are now all citizens of a true city. Still, one woman, Sapia, identifies herself as having been a Sienese. She was filled with envy of her fellow citizens, and rejoiced excessively at their defeat at the hands of the Florentines. Towards the end of her life she repented, but if not for the prayers of a poor comb seller, she would still be in Antepurgatory. She wonders at Dante's presence in Purgatory, for she suspects he is still alive. Dante confirms her feeling, and adds that he will return to have his eyes shut on the terrace of the envious, but only for a short time since he sinned little through envy. He is much more fearful, Dante adds, of the torment below; even now, the burden of pride weighs upon him.

Comment

The envious, having looked with evil eyes on their fellow men, do penance by being denied their sight and forced to rely on the love and support of others. Since the central symbol here is sight, it is fitting that on this terrace Virgil should take guidance from the light of the sun, symbol of the light of God.

CANTO 14

Dante's conversation with Sapia is overheard by two spirits leaning against each other, and they gradually draw him into their talk. They are Guido del Duca, a Ghibelline of Bertinoro, and Rinieri da Calboli, a Guelf of Forli. Asked who he is, Dante declines to answer because his name has no reputation as yet; he also answers the question of his origin by indicating, indirectly, the river Arno. This prompts Guido to launch into an invective against the peoples living along this river, ever more vicious as it flows along until the brutishness met with near its source has come to a **climax** in the treacherous cunning of Florence and Pisa - the Florentines are assigned the rapacity of wolves, and the Pisans the cunning of foxes. This invective ends with a prophecy of the cruelty, in Florence, of Rinieri's grandson, Fulcieri da Calboli. Dante's questioning of the spirits about their own past brings Guido to a second invective, this one directed against the corruption and degeneracy of his own beloved Romagna; he begs Dante to move on and let him weep undisturbed. Virgil and Dante go on their way, to the recitation of examples of envy: Cain, and Aglauros (who was changed to stone because of her jealousy of Mercury's love for her sister).

Comment

Dante's two interlocutors illustrate that citizenship in a truer city referred to by Sapia in the preceding canto. Guido's indignation at the corruption of Tuscany (through which the Arno flows) is all the more compelling because it is not motivated by partisanship, but by the ideals of that heavenly city to which all souls rightly belong. This idealism is corroborated by his anguished denunciation of his own province, the Romagna - both invectives are given the identical number of lines. It is the co-mingling of anger with love, so characteristic of Dante's feeling for Florence, that gives Guido's outburst their moving quality - love becomes wrathful, and wrath becomes pitiful to the Christian idealist who truly loves his country.

The examples of envy underline its self-destructive nature. Cain's envy of his brother alienated him from mankind and terrified him of his fellow men; Aglauros' envy of her sister turned her to stone - i.e., it hardened her nature, destroying all natural feelings in her.

CANTO 15

Virgil and Dante approach the second angel, the angel of fraternal love, who erases the second P from the poet's brow.

The stairway they then mount is far less steep than the others, and as they go up they hear the second Beatitude, "Blessed are the merciful." Dante then asks Virgil to clarify something in Guido's speech in the preceding canto. Guido had reproached mankind for setting its heart where "partnership" is "excluded," and Dante wishes to know what he meant. Virgil explains that the desire for material goods excludes any notion of sharing, and that the more one man possesses, the less there is for others. With spiritual goods, knowledge and especially love, the reverse is true: The more one man has, the more there is for all. If this explanation does not satisfy him, Virgil concludes, let him await further enlightenment from Beatrice.

Conversing thus, the poets reach the third terrace. There, on the terrace of the wrathful, in ecstatic vision, Dante sees examples of meekness - first, the Virgin Mary, meekly reproving the child Jesus for having tarried behind her and Joseph in Jerusalem (Luke ii:43–50); then Pisistratus, ruler of Athens, refusing his wife's demand that he put their daughter's seducer to death; then St. Stephen forgiving the persecutors who are stoning him to death. Waking from his trance, Dante is urged forward by Virgil, and as the two walk towards the evening sun, they are engulfed by a dark cloud of smoke which comes towards them.

Comment

Once he has been cleared of envy by having the second P removed, Dante can begin to understand the nature of Christian fellowship in which all are enriched by the riches of one, a fellowship in grace and charity which envy destroys. By destroying the fellowship linking man to man, it also destroys that greater community which links mankind to God. If Virgil once again refers Dante to Beatrice, it is that this **theme** is central to *Paradiso*, through which she will guide Dante. The more charity there is, the more love descends from heaven, and the more people who love, the more love there is in the universe - God's love, Virgil suggests, increases as man's free will joins it in acts of charity.

As anger is a kind of fog which blinds the mind, the examples of meekness come to Dante in the form of ecstatic visions - the inner illumination contrasting with the inner blindness caused by anger.

PURGATORIO

CANTOS 16-20

. . . .

CANTO 16

The thick fog forces Dante to close his eyes, and led like a blind man by Virgil, he makes his way through the third terrace. He hears the once wrathful spirits sing the Agnus Dei ("Lamb of God"), and is questioned by one of them who realizes that Dante is still alive. Dante informs him of his condition and then asks for his identity. He is Marco Lombardo, a learned Venetian courtier known for his liberality, and he refers, in passing, to the degeneracy of the world. Dante takes this occasion to ask whether that degeneracy is due to the influence of the planets or something inherent in the earth. Marco marvels at such blindness and reminds Dante that man is endowed with free will and is directly dependent on God. The cause of the world's vice is to be found in man, although it is not to be attributed to the corruption of human nature in general. Rather, the disorderly state of the world, Marco insists, is due to the absence of a proper ruler. Rome, he explains, used to have two suns - one lighting the proper way of earthly life, the other lighting the road of God. But now the two lights have quenched each other, as the clergy has grafted the sword onto the crook. The temporal and spiritual powers, confounded together, no longer guide and check one another. The poets now reach the end of the fog; Marco Lombardo points out the angel of meekness and turns back into the mist.

<hr>

Comment

Dante once again takes up the claims of supremacy of the Papacy, to refute them in the name of an ideal social and political order which would regulate the temporal affairs of men just as the Church regulates their spiritual affairs.

Anger, as Dante's experience suggests, blinds one; one must trust to reason and follow its lead if one is to emerge from the fog.

<hr>

CANTO 17

As the poets emerge from the cloud of the wrathful, they look upon the setting sun, and visions of wrath come upon Dante. First he sees Procne, wife of Tereus, who, enraged at her husband's rape of her sister Philomel, killed her son Itys and served him to the father at a meal; she was, according to the legend, changed into a nightingale. Then he sees Haman, who was crucified (so Dante puts it) because of his hatred for Mordecai and the Jews (Esther, iii–vii). Lastly, he sees Lavinia addressing her dead mother Amata, who hanged herself in a fit of frenzy at hearing the news that her daughter's betrothed had been killed by his rival. After these visions, Dante approaches the angel of meekness, who erases the third P from his brow. As they ascend, they hear the third Beatitude. "Blessed are the peacemakers." As they reach the top of the stairs, night falls on their part of the mountain, and Dante finds he cannot move one step further. Straining his ears for any sound in the new circle, Dante hears nothing. He therefore asks Virgil what sin is purged on the fourth terrace, and Virgil tells him that it is sloth.

Virgil takes the opportunity of the enforced rest to discourse further on the general structure of Purgatory. Not only God, but every creature is moved by love, Virgil tells Dante, be that love natural or rational. Natural love can never go astray, but rational love can, either by being misdirected or by being disproportionate - i.e., defective or excessive. When it is directed to primal or secondary good, love cannot lead to sin; but if it is perverse or disproportionate, it is the seed of sin just as it is the source of every virtue when it is in proper measure and rightly directed. Man, Virgil further asserts, cannot hate himself nor his Creator, unless he be a monster; therefore love of evil is always connected with one's neighbor. This is perverse love, which manifests itself as pride, envy, and wrath. The proud one hopes to exalt himself at the expense of his neighbor's abasement; the envious one fears to lose power or whatever else he has set his mind on, and resents any accretion of it to his neighbor; and the wrathful one seeks vengeance through someone else's hurt.

Perverted love, in its three forms, is purged in the three terraces they have just traversed, Virgil tells Dante. Now he will turn his attention to the remaining sections of Purgatory. Defective love, love that is lukewarm, is purged in the terrace they have just reached; it is the realm of the slothful. Finally, Virgil informs his companion, there is a good which is not conducive to happiness, which is not the essence of all good. The love that gives itself over to that good in excess is purged in the remaining three circles, but he will not tell Dante how this love is divided, so that Dante may find it out for himself.

Comment

It is futile to try to reconcile the ethical system here expounded by Virgil with the system of Dante's Hell. One must merely recognize the profound difference in moral climate between the two regions. In Hell the souls are punished for the sins they have committed, but in committing their sins they have committed themselves to evil. In Purgatory, souls are cleansed of their sinfulness, but their ultimate identification is not with the evil or sinful act, but with the grace of God - or else they would not be in Purgatory. In other words, there is a difference between the sin committed out of a dedication - however unconscious - to evil which results from the rejection of God's grace, and the sin committed through error or ignorance which does not reject hope in God. The system of Hell can therefore be drawn from pagan sources - Aristotle and Cicero. The system of Purgatory is part of the traditional system of redemption which Dante, of necessity, had to follow. What Dante contributes to the traditional scheme is the rational ordering of it around the central principle of love, which is the principle of creation. The scheme of Purgatory thus joins the central **theme** of the entire *Divine Comedy*, since it is love which moves Dante on his pilgrimage, the same love which moves the sun and the other stars. Purgatory, in this sense, is a school of love designed to correct the erroneous forms human love has taken.

CANTO 18

Dante's intellectual appetite has only been whetted by Virgil's discourse. He therefore asks his guide to define that love which is the source of all virtue and vice. Love, Virgil explains, is a movement of the mind, which is created with the potential of being attracted to objects it perceives and which please it.

It is a desire, a spiritual movement which rests only when its object "makes it rejoice." In other words, desire can be stilled only by enjoyment of the loved object. Thus it follows that not every act of love is praiseworthy, since not every object is equally worthy.

At this point, Dante introduces an objection. If, he says, love is so totally dependent on outside causes - the objects which arouse the spontaneous desire of the mind, then there is no merit or demerit to the direction the soul takes: Whether for good or for evil, its choice is beyond its control. Having raised the question of free will, Dante listens to Virgil's answer. Virgil first declares that he can enter into the problem only as far as reason can take one; anything beyond that is a question of faith, which Beatrice will be able to answer. There is a prime will, Virgil tells Dante, inherent in the nature of created things, which operates in man in the same way that instinct operates in animals. This will is neither to be praised nor blamed. But man also has free will which, if nothing else, enables him to assent to or reject the choices presented to him by that prime will. Insofar as free will chooses good or evil loves, man is deserving of praise or blame. Those, Virgil says, whose reasoning made them aware of this innate freedom are the ones who gave ethics to the world. In short, even if every desire arises within man out of necessity, man still has the power to control and stop those desires unworthy of him.

It is close to midnight by the time Virgil finishes his discourse, and Dante is dropping off to sleep, when he is suddenly awakened by the rush of the once slothful souls, who now cannot abide to be still. As they run past Dante, they shout examples of zea. Mary's hastening into the country after the Annunciation, and Caesar's race to Spain, from the siege of Marseilles, to battle Pompey's lieutenants. Virgil asks them the way to the next terrace, and an abbot of the monastery of San Zeno, in Verona, shouts back that they should follow behind him. The once slothful cannot rest, so great is their desire to speed. As the last of the slothful pass by, they shout two examples of sloth - the Hebrews who refused to follow Moses and perished in the desert, and the Trojans who would not follow Aeneas and lost all glory. Finally, Dante's thoughts begin to ramble and turn into dreams as he falls asleep.

Comment

Virgil's discourse on the nature of love comes appropriately in the section devoted to the purgation of defective love. It reflects Dante's own interest in the question, since the school of poetry to which he belongs - stilnovism - based its entire system on the notion of the spiritual supremacy of intellectual love. It also gives Dante the occasion to refute the "Epicurean" heresy which maintained that all love was praiseworthy, and which insisted on the inevitability of following one's natural inclination.

The examples of zeal and sloth, drawn from the Bible and pagan antiquity, reveal once again Dante's conception of the two sources of morality in life: the Church, ministering to man's spiritual needs, and the Empire - i.e., law and order - ministering to his temporal needs.

CANTO 19

Toward dawn, Dante dreams of the Siren of classical antiquity whose enchanting song lured sailors to their destruction. The dream comes to him at the coldest part of the early morn, and when the Siren first appears to Dante, she appears a stuttering woman, eyes asquint, crooked on her feet. Dante's gaze suddenly transforms her into a beautiful woman, and she begins to sing so sweetly that she completely absorbs his attention. When she has finished, a lady from heaven suddenly appears who angrily calls Virgil. The latter seizes the Siren, rends her clothes, and exposes her ugliness to Dante. He, overcome by the stench which issues from her belly, awakens to find Virgil by his side, calling him. It is now morning in Purgatory, and the poets approach the angel of zeal who, stroking them with his wings (and presumably erasing another P), pronounces the fourth Beatitude, "Blessed are they that mourn."

As the poets mount to the next terrace, Dante is still preoccupied by his dream; Virgil proceeds to explain it to him. The Siren represents the temptations that have seduced those whose sins are purged in the last three sections of Purgatory; let Dante learn the lesson and turn his eyes from earthly desires to the "lure" placed by God in the heavens above. When they reach the fifth terrace, the poets encounter a host of spirits lying face down on the ground, weeping as they recite "My soul cleaveth unto the dust" (Psalms cxix:25). Once again, Virgil asks the way, and is told to proceed always with the outside of the mountain to his right. The phrasing of the answer - "If you come secure from lying prostrate" - suggests to Dante the law of Purgatory which allows souls to move through any terrace where sins are purged of which they are not guilty. (This law will be illustrated by Statius, who rises from this terrace and moves without impediment through the two that are left.)

Dante then questions the spirit who answered Virgil's question. It is Pope Adrian V, who ruled as pope for little over a month. Until he was made pope, he tells Dante, he was wholly avaricious; when he reached the highest position man can hope for, he suddenly saw the hollowness of worldly ambition and converted his love of earthly things to a love for the life of the spirit. The purgation of the avaricious, he adds, consists in lying outstretched and motionless, eyes fixed to the ground, just as, in their former life, they kept their eyes fixed on earthly things. While Adrian was talking, Dante had knelt, in reverence for his office; the former pope now rebukes him for it, ordering him to stand. In the spirit world, he informs Dante, all souls are equal and fellow-servants of one and the same Power. He then urges Dante to move on and leave him to his weeping.

Comment

Two points worth noting in Dante's dream of the Siren are that it is his gaze which first makes her appear beautiful - a clear instance of that innate freedom of choice not operating properly, and that his absorption is such that a lady from heaven has to set Virgil into action. This feature of the dream corresponds to Dante's actual experience: When he has lost his way, a lady from heaven sends Virgil to his rescue. It may also be taken in conjunction with Dante's fainting at the story of Paolo and Francesca (*Inferno*, Canto 5), and Beatrice's reproof in the earthly paradise (*Purgatorio*, Canto 30). (It has been suggested that Beatrice's strictures refer not so much to Dante's involvement with Philosophy as to other, more natural, lustful loves.) The allegory of the Siren may be cold and mechanical, but the keenness of psychological observation which notes that temptation puts reason to sleep is fully alive.

CANTO 20

Leaving Adrian to his penance, Dante and Virgil press close to the mountainside as they move ahead because the avaricious are so numerous that they fill the terrace to its very edge. The sight of so many distilling through their eyes "the evil that fills the whole world" causes Dante to curse the she-wolf of greed that claims more victims than all the other beasts combined. And Dante asks heaven when will he come, who will finally put her to flight?

Still moving along, Dante hears one of the souls rehearse examples of poverty and liberality. First, as in all the terraces of Purgatory, comes the Virgin Mary, who had to put her child in a stable; then the Roman consul Fabricius, who would not be bribed (Aeneid, vi, 843–844); lastly St. Nicholas, who, according to legend, anonymously provided dowries for the three daughters of a poor neighbor so as to keep them from being driven to a sinful life through poverty. The reciter of these examples is Hugh Capet, founder of the French dynasty, the root, as he puts it, of the evil tree which casts its shadow over all Christian lands. He passes in review some of his more notable descendants and their notorious acts of treachery. He then looks forward to Philip the Fair's attack against the person of the pope, whom he likens to Christ, while Philip is a veritable Pilate. He concludes with a call for vengeance against the infamous French king.

Hugh Capet then explains to Dante that in the morning the once avaricious souls rehearse examples of poverty and generosity, such as the ones he has heard; at night, it is examples of avarice that are rehearsed, and he gives Dante several illustrations. The poets have already parted from the ancestor of the royal line of France, when Dante suddenly feels the entire mountain shake as if in the grips of an earthquake. The fear of death comes over him, and Virgil draws close and tells him not to fear while he guides him. A shout, "Glory to God in the highest," is raised on all sides, and the poets stands motionless until the quake ceases. They then resume their way, greatly puzzled by the event which has just taken place.

Comment

Dante's view of France must be understood in relation to his dream of a truly Holy - i.e., Christian - and truly Roman - i.e., universal - Empire. The unreality of his dream was not apparent to Dante, and he saw in the rising power of France, opposing the national idea to the international idea of Empire, the chief enemy to the political scheme he had outlined in the *De Monarchia*. The idea of a sovereign nation was just barely emerging, and Dante could see in the actions of the French kings, especially Philip the Fair, nothing but a pernicious opposition to both temporal and spiritual law as embodied in the twin institutions of Empire and Church.

It may seem strange that Dante's nemesis, Pope Boniface VIII, should appear in this canto as a second Christ, since Dante elsewhere placed him squarely in Hell. But for once Dante could approve of Boniface's refusal to submit his spiritual authority to the dictates of French policy, and in the assassination of the pope at the instigation of the French king, Dante saw the hand of a temporal ruler raised against the Vicar of Christ. It is because he attacked the spiritual rule of the Church in the person of the pope that King Philip is evil.

PURGATORIO

CANTOS 21-25

. . . .

CANTO 21

As Dante and Virgil continue on their way, they are greeted courteously by a spirit who has come up from behind them. After Virgil explains to the newcomer the nature of Dante's journey, he asks for an explanation of the quake that just passed. The spirit explains that the mountain trembles only when a penitent soul has been cleansed and is ready to rise to Heaven. When a repentent soul finds that its immediate desire, which is to do penance, suddenly coincides with its ultimate desire, which is to reach Heaven, it rises of its own accord and moves up the mountain. The soul's very will to move is assurance that it has been purged. When a soul is thus liberated, the whole mountain shakes and those remaining behind rejoice. The recent quake was due to his own rise after a confinement of five hundred years. He reveals himself as Statius, the Latin poet of the first century A.D., and he expresses his admiration for Virgil, whose Aeneid inspired his own work, an admiration so great that Statius was ready to spend an additional year in Purgatory for the privilege of having lived on earth in Virgil's time. Hearing Statius' words, Virgil, with a look, bids Dante be silent; Dante cannot **refrain** from smiling, however, and his smile leads to the disclosure of Virgil's identity to Statius. Statius immediately falls at Virgil's feet to embrace them, and is checked only by Virgil's reminder that they are both ghosts.

CANTO 22

The three pilgrims, Dante tells us, had already passed the angel of liberality, who erased another P from the poet's brow and who pronounced the fifth Beatitude - "Blessed are they which do ... thirst after righteousness," when Virgil asks Statius how so great a soul as his could have been subject to so puny a vice as avarice. Statius acknowledges the friendly import of the question, but hastens to correct Virgil's impression by declaring that it was prodigality, not avarice, which put him on the fifth terrace of Purgatory: The two opposing sins are there punished together. He adds that he would have been condemned to eternal damnation in Hell for his sin, had he not found a warning against excess in some of Virgil's own lines in the Aeneid. Virgil then further questions him about his conversion to Christianity, since, he says, his writings show no evidence of his having found the true faith. To this inquiry Statius replies that it was again he, Virgil, who lit the path: In Virgil's prophetic fourth Eclogue he found the truth revealed to him. He became a Christian, Statius tells Virgil, and helped succor others of his sect who were persecuted by Rome. His own conversion, however, he kept secret, and his lack of zeal cost him four hundred years on the terrace of the slothful. Statius now asks Virgil about the fate of the great men of antiquity, and Virgil tells him of their state in Limbo.

The three poets have now reached the sixth terrace, and there they come upon a tree laden with apples, but with its shortest branches at the base and its largest branches at the top. A clear spring, dropping from the cliff, waters its leaves. A voice from within the tree calls out "Of this food ye shall have scarcity," and then proceeds to enumerate examples of temperance in eating - the Virgin Mary at the marriage of Cana (also used as an example of generosity in Canto 13), the Roman women of old who abstained from wine, Daniel's rejection of the king's food (Dan., i: 8, 17), and John the Baptist's nourishment of honey and locusts in the wilderness.

Comment

The story of Statius' conversion is Dante's invention and, so far as is known, has no basis in historical fact. At first glance his function is purely **didactic**: It is he who explains things not within the reach of pure reason - the trembling of the mountain, and the process of liberation from sin, which is an operation of the individual conscience working in harmony with divine justice.

But Statius has a dramatic function as well. To the pagan poet Virgil, supremely endowed with rational morality, is superimposed the Christian poet Statius with his intimate knowledge - intimate because he has experienced it - of the workings of grace. The supreme **irony** is that Statius' state of grace is due to Virgil's teaching; without Virgil's fourth Eclogue (which in the Middle Ages was read as a prophecy of the coming of Christ) Statius would not even have achieved the relatively painless station Virgil occupies in Limbo. Dante obviously intends Statius as a Christian Virgil (Statius is present throughout the proceedings in the earthly paradise, whereas

Virgil can only lead Dante to its threshold), but through Statius Dante pays his greatest tribute to Virgil: When he has Statius turn to Virgil and exclaim "Through thee I was poet, through thee a Christian," the words may be the Latin poet's but the feeling of indebtedness and gratitude is clearly Dante's.

Still, the moral point is not lost sight of. Insofar as Statius is the fulfillment of the promise held out by Virgil, his presence in *Purgatorio* is yet one more indication of the fact that reason's ultimate justification is not in itself, but in faith.

CANTO 23

As the poets proceed, they are overtaken by the once gluttonous spirits, all of whom are now emaciated images of thirst and starvation. They are nothing but skin and bones, and they sing "O Lord, open thou my lips; and my mouth shall show forth thy praise" (Psalms, 1i:15). Dante wonders how the tree and the stream can work such results on the shadowy forms. One of them addresses Dante, and Dante recognized him by the voice, for he would never have recognized him by his appearance. It is his old friend Forese Donati, who explains that he and his fellow-sinners are purged by hunger and thirst; the trees and the stream, by increasing their desire for food and drink, increase their torment, and thus their solace, since they thus crucify the appetites of the flesh in them.

Having understood the penance of the sixth terrace, Dante expresses his surprise at finding Forese there instead of in Antepurgatory with the late-repentant. Forese replies that his being in Purgatory is due to the devotion of his widow Nella. Her virtue, he tells Dante, is all the dearer to God in that it shines more brightly when set against the vices of the other Florentine women. After a brief attack on the brazen immodesty of the women of Florence, Forese begs Dante to relate his story. Dante briefly reminds Forese of the quality of their life when they were companions on earth, and adds that Virgil came to rescue him from that life. He has been led through Hell and up the mountain of Purgatory, and soon he will be led to Beatrice. There, when he meets her, he will lose his present guide.

Comment

The encounter with Forese Donati is drawn from an obscure part of Dante's biography. He and Forese were apparently youthful friends who exchanged some highly scurrilous **sonnets** in exceedingly vulgar taste; these suggest (though they by no means prove) a riotous, debauched life. (One must not forget the possibility that these poems were nothing more than a high-spirited game, albeit in poor taste.) It has also been suggested that Dante put Forese in Purgatory, and had him praise his widow, by way of making amends for one **sonnet** in which the avowed lover of Beatrice mocks Nella coarsely for her husband's unfaithfulness. The one thing that is certain is that some personal experience of the past is involved, since Forese is the only person to whom Dante mentions Beatrice without any sort of explanation.

Again one must beware of confusing the hero of the poem with the author; one must not read the *Divine Comedy* as if it were a collection of notes for an autobiography. Whatever the facts of Dante's companionship with Forese may have been, the suggestion made in this canto is deliberate: a morally dissolute life from which the poet was rescued by Virgil so that he might find Beatrice; the context of Forese's praise for his widow and attack against the loose morals of Florentine woman, and Dante's mention of Beatrice point to such an interpretation. Dante does not need to expose whatever moral turpitude he may have in mind. It is enough that he suggests it to bring the nature of his pilgrimage into relief.

CANTO 24

The last person Dante has identified in the preceding canto has been Statius, and Dante now adds the thought that perhaps Statius delays his upward journey for the sake of Virgil. He then inquires of Forese about the fate of his sister Piccarda, and he is told that she is already in heaven. Forese next points out some fellow spirits, among whom is the poet Bonagiunta of Lucca, who propheries Dante's pleasant reception in Lucca at the hands of a women named Gentucca. But, Bonagiunta continues. "Do I really see before me the man who brought forth the new **rhymes** beginning with 'Ladies that have intelligence of love?'" "I am one who," answers Dante, "when love inspires me, take note, and set it forth in the manner in which he dictates within me." Having heard this answer, Bonagiunta declares himself satisfied: He now understands the principle of the sweet new style which baffled not only him, but the Notary (Jacopo da Lentino) and Guittone (Guittone d' Arezzo). Dante and his school of poetry followed the dictates of love in their writing as these other poets did not. And, he adds by way of conclusion, there is no further difference to be sought between the two schools.

The throng of spirits now quickens its pace; only Forese stays behind, to ask Dante when he will see him again. Dante does not know how much longer he will live, but his spirit is already eager to come to the bank of the Tiber, especially as his city, Florence, degenerates day by day and seems doomed to ruin. Forese thereupon ascribes the misery of Florence to his brother

Corso, whose death and damnation he predicts. And then Forese leaves Dante to rush after the throng of penitent spirits.

The poets next come upon a second tree like the one they have already seen. This one, they are told by a voice from the foliage, is a shoot from the tree of the knowledge of good and evil from which Eve plucked the apple. The voice then rehearses various examples of gluttony; after hearing these, the poets march in silence until they come to the angel of temperance, glowing in a red light that quite blinds Dante. The angel erases the sixth P from Dante's brow, and recites a paraphrase of the Beatitude. "Blessed are they which do hunger ... after righteousness," which constitutes the sixth Beatitude in Purgatory.

Comment

The literary discussion between Bonagiunta and Dante may seem strangely out of place in the ethical scheme of *Purgatorio*, but it has a relevance which reaches beyond the proper critical distinction between two schools of poetry. Much discussion has been occasioned by Dante's definition of stilnovism, the "sweet new style" referred to by Bonagiunta. (The term "stilnovism" comes from this passage; the original for "sweet new style" is "dolce stil nuovo.") The literary issue really boils down to a question of sincerity - the poets of the sweet new style disclaim the artificiality of the older school of love poetry in favor of direct inspiration. Dante says that he merely sets forth what love dictates within him. This distinction between the two schools of poetry has a direct bearing on Dante's undertaking in *the Divine Comedy*, however. For if poetry is a means to attain and express truth, then it must be attuned to the source of truth, which is God. The love which inspires Dante is the Holy Spirit, then; it is a supernatural source of inspiration which dictates to the poet just as it does to the prophet. Virgil's discourses on the fourth terrace (Cantos 17 and 18) have treated of love as it manifests itself in human experience; Dante now asserts its reality as the source of truth. The theme that will be orchestrated and developed in *Paradiso* begins to make itself heard in Purgatory as the poets get closer to the earthly paradise.

CANTO 25

On their way to the seventh terrace Dante wonders how the souls of the gluttonous can suffer the physical pangs of thirst and hunger when they have no bodies requiring nourishment. Virgil refers him to Statius for an explanation. Statius thereupon exposes the theory of generation. The purest part of a man's blood, Statius declares, is not absorbed into the bloodstream, but set aside and endowed by the heart with the power of giving form to all human organs and members; thus refined it descends into the organs of generation. When it is joined to the woman's blood in the act of generation, the fusion produces a new substance which goes through three stages of development, a development conditioned by the "active" virtue of the male seed (the woman's is disposed to passivity). This active virtue at first becomes a soul akin to that possessed by plants. In other words, in the first stage of development, the new substance takes on the life of a plant endowed with what was termed a vegetative soul. Next it acquires sensation and motion; the organism takes on animal life under the direction of the animal soul. Finally, when the articulation of the brain is complete in the embryo, God infuses into it the rational soul, which distinguishes human beings from brute animals. This new soul absorbs into itself the faculties of the vegetative and animal souls which preceded it; the result is a single soul which lives, feels, and revolves around itself. This is the human soul which is immortal; this is the soul which, at the time of death, leaves the body, carrying within itself all the potential that makes a human being. When it lands near either the Acheron or the Tiber, it creates around itself an ethereal semblance out of the surrounding air. Out of that form, or shade, it then creates all the sensory organs, including that of sight. In this way the spirits can show all the reactions of living bodies.

The poets have now reached the last terrace, and they turn their attention to other concerns. The terrace is filled with flames, except for a narrow passage near the edge, and Dante proceeds cautiously along that passage, fearing the fire on one side and the drop on the other. He hears the lustful sing from within the fire the hymn, "God of highest clemency," which contains a prayer against lust. They then recite examples of chastity - the Virgin Mary's expression of surprise at the Annunciation, since she knows no man, and the virgin moon - goddess Diana's dismissal of one of her nymphs who had borne a son to Jupiter. Resuming their chanting for a while, they return to examples of chastity, calling out wives and husbands who were chaste within wedlock. Such, Dante says, is the treatment which heals the last wound.

Comment

Statius' disquisition may again strike us as a piece of pedantry, but since the last three terraces cleanse sins of the flesh, the relationship of body to soul may be properly explored. It is significant that here again, where the Christian view dominates, Virgil defers to his Christian counterpart.

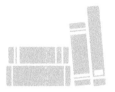

PURGATORIO

CANTOS 26-29

. . . .

CANTO 26

Dante's body casts a shadow on the flames, and the souls gather to gaze at him, being careful to stay within the fire. One spirit asks Dante the reason for his being there, but before the poet can reply another group arrives, exchanges kisses with the first, and both recite examples of lust - Sodom and Gomorrah, and Pasiphae. After the new group has gone, Dante explains the nature of his journey, and in turn asks for an explanation what he has just witnessed. He is told by the spirit who first spoke to him that the recently arrive group contained those guilty of abnormal lust - i.e., homosexuals, who therefore cried "Sodom and Gomorrah," while those in the first group were guilty of following their lust like brute beasts, without observing human law. The speaker then identifies himself as Guido Guinizelli, the founder, or at least precursor, of the sweet new style. Dante expresses his respect and admiration for his "father," but Guido points to the troubadour poet Arnaut Daniel as a better craftsman. With a request for Dante's prayers, he yields his place to Daniel who, speaking in Provencal, discloses his state and asks to be remembered by Dante.

Comment

The examples of chastity proclaimed in the preceding canto are drawn from both Christian and pagan tradition. But lest chastity be confused with an unnatural requirement for total abstinence, the once lustful souls sing the praises not only of the Virgin Mary and Diana, but of chaste husbands and wives who kept their sexual appetite within the bonds of marriage. The groups of sinners kiss as a token of the purity of affection no longer tainted by lust, and the examples they recite are reminders of sexual perversion and loss of human control over passion, respectively.

CANTO 27

The three poets come to the angel of chastity, who pronounces the seventh Beatitude - "Blessed are the pure in heart." The angel then informs them that to proceed further they must go through the fire; this news terrifies Dante who stands with clasped hands gazing at the flames and recalling the sight of men he has seen burned to death. Virgil tries to reassure him. reminding him of the other frightening moments of their journey, but to no avail; only when he mentions Beatrice does Dante finally agree to move. Virgil enters first and asks Statius to come last, so that Dante may be between them. The heat, Dante says, was so intense that he would have flung himself into molten glass to cool off; all the while, Virgil speaks to him of Beatrice to give him courage. Guided by a voice from the other side of the flames, the poets finally emerge to be greeted with the words to be spoken to the righteous at the Last Judgment: "Come, ye blessed of my Father"

(Matt, xxv:34). As the sun sets, the poets settle for the night on the stairs leading to the Garden of Eden, and Dante falls asleep. Towards dawn he dreams of Leah and Rachel; Leah is gathering flowers with which to adorn herself, and she speaks of her sister Rachel, who sits all day gazing at the reflection of her eyes in a mirror. Leah then explains that while her sister takes pleasure in contemplation, she finds satisfaction in action.

When Dante awakens in the morning, Virgil tells him he is about to obtain that fruit of liberty he has been seeking; and, indeed, Dante finds that his desire to mount to the top of the stairs is so strong that at every step he seems to be taking flight. At the top step Virgil speaks to Dante for the last time. He has brought Dante this far, he says, with art and reason; now Dante may take his pleasure for a guide. He, Virgil, can do no more for Dante. Dante's will is now free, upright, and whole; he must now act as it prompts him. Therefore, Virgil concludes, Dante now holds the crown and mitre over himself.

Comment

As the tradition of the Church had made the flaming sword which guarded the Garden of Eden after the Fall into a wall of fire encircling the earthly paradise, Dante uses the fire on the seventh terrace both as purgation for lust and as that encircling wall which all souls must pass through. In Dante's case, of course, we must take his fear of the fire as an indication of his participation in the sin it is designed to cleanse; consequently he feels its heat in a way we gather neither Virgil nor Statius do.

Dante's dream projects traditional medieval images of the active and the contemplative life - for so were the two wives of Jacob, Leah and Rachel, allegorized. Here they foreshadow the two ladies Dante will shortly encounter: Matilda, the genius of the earthly paradise, who, like Leah, will be gathering flowers and singing, and Beatrice, who will lead Dante on his journey through Paradise.

Virgil's final words to Dante indicate that Dante has reached the goal for which Church and Empire were designed: He is now king and bishop over himself. (In the *De Monarchia* Dante indicated that Church and Empire were necessitated by the Fall, and that man in his state of innocence did not need such institutions to direct him.) Dante can now follow his pleasure as guide because, his soul having been cleansed of sin, his pleasure will automatically be in harmony with the divinely established moral order.

CANTO 28

Dante enters the Garden of Eden and wanders until he reaches a stream, on the other side of which he sees a lady gathering flowers as she sings. In answer to Dante's request, she approaches the stream from her side; as she looks up, her smile awakens a response of rapture in Dante's heart. She is the genius of the place, and she refers Dante and his companions to Psalm 112 ("For thou, Lord, hast made me glad through thy work") for an explanation of her smiling. In answer to a question from Dante, she explains that the higher regions of the mountain are not subject to changes in the weather; that the breeze he feels is caused by the sweep of the airy envelope of the earth, moving from east to west with the Primum Mobile; that the stream rises from a fountain which finds its source in the will of God. That fountain actually feeds two streams: On the one side is Lethe, which washes away the memory of sin, and on the other is Eunoe, which restores the memory of good deeds. Finally, she says, those who in ancient times sang of a golden age of man perhaps were dreaming of this earthly paradise; for here man was innocent, here reigns an eternal spring, here is found every conceivable fruit. At these words, Dante turns to look at his poets, as he calls them, and sees that their faces have lit up with a smile of recognition.

Comment

The lady appearing on the other side of Lethe is Matilda (so named by Beatrice in Canto 32), who is the fulfillment of the vision of Leah in Dante's dream. In *the De Monarchia* (III, xvi, 43–52) Dante has said that God has set two ends before man: "the blessedness, to wit, of this life, which consists in the exercise of his proper power and is figured by the terrestrial paradise, and the blessedness of eternal life, which consists in the fruition of the divine aspect, to which his proper power may not ascend unless assisted by the divine light. And this blessedness is given to be understood by the celestial paradise." Here Matilda represents the blessedness of this life, a blessedness that manifests itself in action. She goes one step further than Leah, however; for Leah merely rejoiced in the work of God's hands, hence the reference to the psalm. Dante has been cleansed of sin, and has thus been able to reach the Garden of Eden; he has yet to learn the lesson of the Garden and perfect himself accordingly before he can rise to the "blessedness of eternal life" which is to be understood "by the celestial paradise." It is this final earthly education to which the remaining cantos of *Purgatorio* are devoted.

CANTO 29

Chanting a blessing on those whose sins have been covered up, Matilda resumes her walk along the bank of the stream, and

Dante keeps pace with her on his side. They are now facing east, and Matilda bids Dante look and listen. He sees a dazzling bright light in the forest and hears music in the air, so sweet that his indignation is aroused at the thought that Eve's action robbed him and mankind of this abode. The bright light approaches, and he begins to discern details as he also hears a resounding "Hosanna." Amazed at what he sees, he turns to Virgil, whose face expresses no less amazement than his. Dante therefore turns back to the approaching spectacle. As he glances into the stream on his left, he sees the reflection of his left side in it; he then places himself in position to observe the divine pageant of revelation that is approaching.

First come seven gold candlesticks, the flames of which form seven streamers the colors of the rainbow, the outermost of which are ten paces apart. Behind them come twenty-four elders clad in white, crowned with lilies. They are followed by four winged beasts, each having six wings full of eyes, and each crowned with green leaves. Their form, Dante says, will be found described in Ezekiel. These four surround a triumphal car on two wheels drawn by a griffin, whose wings, stretching through the middle bands made by the flaming streamers, cover them equally and stretch into the sky. The bird part of the griffin is of gold; the rest is white mingled with red. At the right wheel of the car are three ladies dancing in a round; one is red, the other green, and the third white, and the white and red ladies alternately lead the dance, but they always take their cue from the song of the red one. At the left wheel Dante sees four ladies clad in purple, one of whom, the leader, has three eyes in her head. The procession is brought to a close by two venerable-looking elders, followed by four others of lowly mien, followed by one old man seemingly in a trance. These seven, like the twenty-four elders seen before, are also clad in white. Instead of being crowned with lilies, however, they are crowned with roses and other red flowers, so that they seem on fire above the eyes. A loud thunderclap is heard as the car comes opposite to where Dante stands, and the procession comes to a halt.

Comment

The pageant of revelation is of necessity supernatural and symbolic. Its **imagery** is drawn from the Old and New Testaments as they were interpreted and understood in the Middle Ages. The seven candlesticks represent the seven gifts of the Holy Spirit: wisdom, understanding, counsel, might, knowledge, pity, and fear of God. The seven streamers have been variously interpreted as the seven sacraments of the Church, or the working of the seven gifts. Dante's specific notation of the fact that the outside streamers are ten paces apart may be a reference to the Ten Commandments. The twenty-four elders clad in white indicate the twenty-four books of the Old Testament (so arranged in the Vulgate of St. Jerome); the white color of their raiment represents faith, and the crowns of lilies, purity.

The four-winged beasts about the car - in the forms of man, lion, ox, and eagle - are familiar medieval symbols of the Evangelists (Matthew, Mark, Luke, and John). They are crowned with the symbol of hope (green leaves), and the six wings represent the six laws - natural, Mosaic, prophetic, evangelical, Apostolic, and canonical. The eyes in the wings suggest their knowledge of past and future. The triumphant car itself is the Church Militant in its ideal state; the two wheels have been variously interpreted as the active and contemplative life, the Old and New Testaments, or the Franciscan and Dominican orders which sought love and knowledge, respectively.

(In *Paradiso*, Canto 12, St. Francis and St. Dominic are called the wheels of the chariot in which the Church defends herself.) The griffin, part eagle and part lion, represents the twofold nature of Christ - divine and human at once; the gold part stands for his divinity, the white and red for his humanity. Its two wings, which reach to heaven, are believed to stand for mercy and justice.

The three ladies by the right-hand wheel are the three theological virtues: Faith (white), Hope (green), and Charity or Love (red). The four beside the other wheel are the moral virtues, dressed in purple, the color of empire, and led by one of them, Prudence (hence the three eyes). The others are Justice, Fortitude or Courage, and Temperance.

Lastly, the seven elders who bring up the rear represent the remaining books of the New Testament. First Luke (as author of the Acts of the Apostles) and Paul; then the writers of the General Epistles, James, Peter, John, and Jude; and finally John, the visionary author of Revelation.

The pageant thus reveals in one tableau the perfect picture of the Church Militant designed for the guidance of mankind.

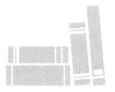

PURGATORIO

CANTOS 30-33

. . . .

CANTO 30

When the car has stopped, the elders all turn to it, and one of them invokes the bride of Lebanon (Song of Songs, iv:8). Spirits arise, shouting "Blessed art thou who comest," and "Oh, with full hands give lilies," and a lady appears, dressed in white, green, and red, and crowned with olive-leaves. Dante at once recognizes Beatrice and, frightened, looks for Virgil. But Virgil has gone, and all the joys of the earthly paradise cannot keep Dante from weeping at his loss. Beatrice, calling him by his name, bids him not to weep for Virgil, for there are other things he must weep for. She then bids him look at her, and asks how he has presumed to come to this mountain. Dante, like a child, looks down, but seeing himself reflected in the stream, quickly looks away and stares at the grass, feeling full of shame. His heart is frozen; he is unable to feel. But the sound of angels interceding for him with Beatrice melts him and he begins to sob as the tears gush forth from his eyes.

Beatrice remains unbending, however. Turning to the angelic presences, she speaks of the promise of Dante's youth, and of his betrayal of that promise after her death. For a while, she says, she sustained him with her presence; but once she died, he forsook her and pursued false visions of good. He sank so low, says Beatrice, that the only way left to save him was to make him see Hell for himself; for his sake, then, did she go and beseech Virgil to guide him hither. God's high decree, she concludes, demands that the penitence of tears be paid before the memory of such sin be erased by the river Lethe.

CANTO 31

Turning to Dante once again, Beatrice declares that his confession must be joined to her accusation. Dante is at first tongue-tied, then forces out a weak "Yes," so weak that one has to look at him to understand what he is saying. But Beatrice persists. She wants Dante to tell her what deflected him from his path of true love for her, and a weeping Dante answers that the allurement of present beauties drew him as soon as her face was hidden (i.e., as soon as she died). This reply occasions further reproof: If anything, Beatrice tells him her death should have taught him the vanity and emptiness of earthly things. As he still looks down, she reminds him that he is a man, not a child, and calls on him to look up at her. Obeying with great difficulty, Dante is so stung by remorse that his conscience can no longer bear the burden and he falls senseless to the ground.

When he comes to, Dante finds himself immersed up to his neck in the river Lethe. He is drawn across by Matilda, who then plunges his head under and makes him drink of the water. Pulling him out, Matilda leads him into the circle of the four ladies clad in purple. These tell him that they are Beatrice's hand-maidens, and that they will lead him to her eyes. They will only lead him to Beatrice's eyes; it is the three dancing on the other side of the car, whose gaze goes deeper than theirs, who will strengthen him to gaze into those eyes. They lead him to the griffin and bid him look on the eyes of his lady. Beatrice, however, keeps her gaze firmly fixed on the griffin, and Dante can see, through the veil, the double nature of the beast reflected in them. Although the griffin itself remains unchanged, Beatrice's eyes now show the attributes of one nature, now the attributes of the other.

While Dante's soul is drinking in the sight, the other three ladies come forward to urge Beatrice to turn her eyes on her faithful lover, and to unveil her mouth so that he may see her smile. No one, Dante exclaims, can do justice to the resplendence of eternal living light revealed to him at that moment.

Comment

Cantos 30 and 31 are a superb example of the way in which Dante fuses the public aspect of events with the intensely personal psychological experience these events produce. The pageant of Canto 29 is a public demonstration of the Church Militant and the mystery of Revelation. This public manifestation takes on an intimately personal meaning in these two cantos. Revelation as an abstract notion is well and good, and interesting in its own right, but it will be without fruit if it does not at the same time reveal the man to himself. This **theme** is already hinted at in the 29th canto, when Dante catches a glimpse of his left side - his impure side - in the river Lethe; it is confirmed in Canto 30 when, looking down because of the sting of Beatrice's reproof, he accidentally sees himself reflected in the river and quickly shifts his gaze to the grass. Dante is perfectly willing to look at a pageant of Revelation; but to took at himself, to face himself with all his failings is more than he is at first willing to do. He seeks refuge in childlike excuses and tears; Beatrice has to force him to face up to himself, and then the guilt becomes so intense that he escapes by fainting.

His loss of consciousness is a measure of his sense of guilt for having abandoned the pure love of Beatrice for lesser loves of this world (whatever specific offense Dante may have in mind is immaterial). But it is also the guarantee of his spiritual rebirth, and when he is reborn (when he comes to), he is already being immersed in the river which washes away the memory of sin - in other words, the burden of guilt is lifted from him. Now he can prepare himself for the fuller revelation to be found in Beatrice's eyes, to which he is led by the four mortal virtues which lead man to the threshold of earthly perfection. But to gaze into those eyes, to look, unflinching, at the light revealed in them, he needs the strength of the theological virtues - Faith, Hope, and Charity. Only these purely Christian virtues can give him the strength to sustain the reflection of God's light. To see the mystery of the Incarnation, the moral virtues were sufficient. But to see the reflection of God Himself requires the support of those other more profound virtues (the four ladies tell Dante that their three sisters gaze more deeply than they do). Dante's experience with Beatrice's eyes anticipates the process of ascent in *Paradiso*, where Dante is repeatedly strengthened to sustain the increasingly intense light of the heavens.

CANTO 32

The intensity of his gaze into Beatrice's eyes leaves Dante momentarily blinded when his face is turned away by the three ladies who tell him he is staring too fixedly. He must now readjust his sight to lesser objects. The procession is moving once again, and Dante and Statius, led by Matilda, take their place by the right wheel of the car. They move through the forest, deserted since Adam's day, and come to a tree despoiled of its foliage, and all the members of the procession murmur "Adam!" The griffin does reverence to the tree, the pole of the car is bound to the tree, and the tree suddenly bursts into bloom. He now falls asleep, and awakens bewildered, to find Beatrice sitting on the ground, surrounded by the seven ladies, each of whom holds one of the seven candlesticks.

Beatrice informs Dante of his mission - he is to report to the world what he is about to witness. What he witnesses are allegorical portrayals of the disasters which have befallen the Church in its history. First an eagle swoops down on the tree, rends its bark and foliage, and then smites the car, making it reel to and fro. Then a she-fox leaps into the car; it is chased away by Beatrice. Next, the eagle comes down a second time and leaves the car covered with its feathers; a voice then cries out bemoaning the load put on the car. Then Dante sees the ground between the two wheels open, and a dragon emerges that spikes its tail through the car and wrenches out a part of the bottom before going on its way. What is left of the chariot now covers itself with the feathers. Next it acquires seven heads, three double-horned heads over the pole, and four single-horned heads at the corners. A harlot appears seated on it, a giant at her side; from time to time the two kiss. But as the harlot begins to eye Dante, the giant, after beating her, looses the seven-headed monster and leads it off into the forest till it is out of sight.

Comment

In this canto Dante returns to the public allegory of Canto 29. The three theological virtues reproach him for staring too fixedly at

Beatrice because, while she is the revelation of God's truth for Dante, she is also the reflection of God's light for the world, and must take her place at the center of the pageant of the Church Militant. The pageant has a public purpose which goes beyond Dante's personal feelings for Beatrice, or, for that matter, for God. The show must go on to make its demonstration, and it is Dante's job, as Beatrice tells him, to record what he sees and report it to the world. To Dante, of course, this means adjusting his vision from greater to lesser things, since for him Beatrice is all the demonstration that he needs.

What Dante then witnesses is an allegory of the relation of Church and Empire. The tree, which is the tree of knowledge of good and evil, represents the Empire because it embodies the principle of law and obedience; had Adam and Eve respected this principle, there would have been no need for either Empire or Church. The griffin, representing Christ in his human incarnation, obeys law by respecting the tree, and reveals the nature of the relationship between the two great institutions of the West by tying the car of the Church to the tree of Empire. It is a relationship of reciprocity that is desired, not of supremacy for one or the other: No sooner is the car tied to the tree than the tree recovers its foliage. But once again, this demonstration proclaims the ideal, and the world lives in time with the passage of which institutions and relationships change. When Dante awakens from his slumber, only Beatrice is left to guard the car of the Church with the help of the seven virtues holding the seven gifts of the Holy Spirit (see Canto 29, Comment).

The second part of the allegory concerns the falling off from the proper relationship between Church and Empire, told in terms of disasters that befell the Church. The first descent of the eagle represents the persecution of the early Church by the Roman emperors; the she-fox, heresies which threatened the early Church and which were suppressed by the writings of the Church Fathers; the second descent of the eagle, the "donation of Constantine," which supposedly turned the temporal rule of the Western Empire over to the Papacy. The dragon stands for the schism wrought by Mahomet; the further bedecking of the car with feathers, the enrichment of the Church by the medieval emperors Pepin and Charlemagne; the sprouting of the heads, the consequent corruption and transformation of the Church, now bedecked with the seven deadly sins. Lastly, the harlot represents the contemporary Papacy - that of Boniface VIII and Clement V, and the giant represents the French dynasty, specifically Philip the Fair. It was with his connivance that Clement V transferred the Papal See to Avignon, an action represented by the giant's dragging the harlot and the monster off with himself. The point of this elaborate allegory is that the Church Militant, so glorious in its appearance when it was wedded to Revelation, has now become a corrupt monster and is endangering its mission.

CANTO 33

After the spoliation of the car, the seven ladies alternately cry out "O God, the heathen are come into thine inheritance," and Beatrice herself looks as altered as Mary at the Cross. But she rises to her feet, and, using the words of Christ, tells the ladies that for a while she will be withdrawn from their sight but in a while they will see her again. She then places them in front of her, and signals to Dante, Matilda, and Statius to follow behind. Before taking her tenth step, however, she calls Dante to her side and invites him to question her. He, still shy, tells her that she knows his needs and what is good for him.

Beatrice then launches into a prophecy about the future of the Church and the Empire which is couched in very obscure terms. First, she tells Dante, the vessel which the serpent broke, was, and is not; but God's vengeance will catch up with the one who is at fault. Secondly, the eagle that left its plumage in the car will not be without heir for long; she can see in the stars that a 515, sent by God, will slay the harlot and the giant who sins with her. Perhaps, she adds, her prophecy is not clear; but the riddle, she adds, will be solved. She then discourses briefly of the tree, which, she says, has been despoiled twice. Whoever robs it offends God; and if Dante were not so sluggish of mind, he would recognize God's justice in the prohibition against taking anything from that tree. But as his mind is turned to stone, it is her will that he bear her words with him, if only in outline, to show that he has been in the earthly paradise.

Dante asks her why her words go over his head, when he is ready to have his mind stamped by her. So that he may see, she replies, how inadequately his philosophic studies have prepared him for understanding her. At this point Dante claims to have no recollection of ever having estranged himself from her. Beatrice smiles, and points out the fact that since he drank from Lethe all recollection of sinful acts has been wiped out; therefore, the estrangement must have been sinful since he cannot recall it. But from now on, she adds, her words to him will be clear.

By this time they have come to the fountain which divides itself into two streams, and Dante marvels at the sight. Beatrice tells him to ask Matilda about it, and Matilda denies any fault on her part since she told Dante all about that fountain earlier. Furthermore, she is sure that Lethe cannot have made him forget that information. Beatrice replies that his intense spiritual experience may have caused this lapse of memory. At any rate, she adds, let Matilda now take him to Eunoe. At these words Matilda takes Dante by the hand and tells Statius to follow. And Dante concludes by saying that he returned from that stream born anew, pure, and ready to mount to the stars.

Comment

The wrongs inflicted on the Church are, to Beatrice, like a new Crucifixion, and she is consequently moved as was Mary at the foot of the Cross. The visible Church is absent, and Beatrice is now the true soul of the Church, and even she, like Christ, will disappear from view for a short while.

Turning to Dante, she wants him to fulfill his mission of bringing word of the spoliation of the Church back to mankind, and she interprets the allegorical scenes they have witnessed in terms that are more obscure than the scenes themselves. Beatrice in 1300 is prophecying events that were contemporaneous with Dante's writing of these pages, the outcome of which may not have been clear. The number 515 follows the Hebrew custom of assigning numbers to various letters and expressing a name through numbers.

This particular number is generally interpreted as an anagram of DUX, the Latin word meaning "leader": In the Roman numeral system D is 500, X is ten, and V (interchangeable with U) is 5. Dante probably had Henry VII of Luxembourg in mind, since Beatrice refers to the eagle's not remaining without an heir (in Dante's mind the emperors who followed Frederick II were not true emperors since they never came into Italy and were not crowned in Rome). For our purposes it is enough to know that Dante, through Beatrice, is still keeping to his dream of a truly international State of law and order. This ideal is symbolized, as we have seen, by the forbidden tree; in the prohibition, Beatrice tells Dante, one can recognize God's righteousness. Man's righteousness is similarly founded in the willing obedience of the prohibition. The whole social purpose of *Purgatorio* is to demonstrate the need for justice and order in civil society, because where anarchy reigns, where power is a servant of greed, man cannot live freely and at peace on what Dante has termed, in the *De Monarchia*, "this threshing-floor of mortals." The state of the world not only robs man of "the blessedness of this life," but it also puts him in peril of losing the "blessedness of eternal life." It is this blessedness that the stream Eunoe prepares him for by strengthening the memory of all good. Cleansed in his soul, armed with the memory of good, he is now ready to ascend to the stars.

PARADISO

Since the structure of Dante's *Paradiso* has already been discussed (see Introduction), a brief restatement of its main features is all that is needed here. The earth's atmosphere is surrounded by a region of fire, beyond which are found nine concentric spheres making up the cosmos which exists in space and time. These spheres are the so-called planetary heavens which revolve around the earth. They are, in order of ascent, the Moon, Mercury, Venus, the Sun, Mars, Jupiter, Saturn, the Stellar Heaven of Fixed Stars, and the Primum Mobile. Beyond these lies the Empyrean, the region of the infinite and the eternal, where God resides with his angels and the redeemed.

The redeemed reside with God in the Empyrean, but their souls manifest themselves in the various planetary heavens, according to the virtue which ruled their lives. Thus the Moon shows the Inconstant, those whose souls were directed toward faith, but toward an earth-tainted and therefore imperfect faith. Similarly, Mercury is set aside for the Active or Ambitious - souls whose hope in god drove them to a life of action in this world. Venus holds the souls of the Amarous, whose love was of necessity less than perfect since they were human beings and not God. The first three heavens therefore manifest the souls of those who governed their lives in accordance with the three theological virtues of Faith, Hope, and Charity, but who fell short of absolute perfection in these virtues because men are earthlings and not pure spirit.

Psychologically, the three theological virtues are experienced by human beings as feelings. The four planetary heavens above these three manifest virtues derived from the moral conscience rather than from the emotions - the cardinal or moral virtues of Prudence (or Wisdom), Fortitude (or Courage), Justice, and Temperance, found respectively in the Sun, Mars, Jupiter, and Saturn. These seven - the three theological and the four cardinal virtues - complete the roster of human virtue. The next two heavens take us to an entirely different plane - the theological virtues no longer felt as emotional impulse by man, but revealed as objective truth in the universe. In other words, the Stellar Heaven and the Primum Mobile show Faith and Hope as spiritual realities of the universe rather than just feelings experienced by man. The Stellar Heaven is the realm of the souls, the realm in which the triumph of redemption is manifested; it reveals the power of Faith, necessary for salvation. The Primum Mobile, the heaven which through its motion moves all the other heavens, is expressive of the Hope of the entire order of Creation. It is the realm of the angels, who do not need faith for salvation. Rather, they live in constant hope of God's love.

So far, the structure of Dante's cosmos reveals the universe's dependence on God; it is linked to God through Faith and Hope. But the link is a two-way proposition: God is not only the source of all creation. He is also its goal. It is in the tenth heaven, the Empyrean, that the promise held out by faith and hope is fulfilled. There God is revealed as Infinite Love (Charity) the motivating force which brought about creation and which draws the created universe back to Itself. There the ultimate mystery of the universe is not so much explained as experienced.

A few words about the nature of the vision in *Paradiso* are in order. The vision in *Inferno* is realistic and dramatic: Dante's Hell is a stage, so to speak, on which is acted out for all eternity the conflict between man's fallen nature and God's will. The consequence of that conflict is damnation. The tone of *Purgatorio* is **didactic**, rather than dramatic. In Purgatory the dominant issue is no longer the drama of man's damnation, but the painstaking process of purgation. This process is essentially educative: Informed by grace and guided by moral reason, man learns to perfect himself in order to regain the earthly paradise that was lost by the Fall. The focus is on human experience. The learning process takes place in a realm of light and shade which is a reflection of, and commentary on, the world of the living. In *Paradiso*, on the other hand, Dante leaves the world of earthly reality behind to move onto the plane of **metaphysical** truth. Dante's Paradise is a completely spiritual realm, even, as we have seen, in its physical aspect.

Since human reason is not capable of effecting the final purification of the soul, it certainly cannot guide Dante through the realm of pure spirit. Here God must take over, and it is He who, through the agency of Beatrice, will reveal to Dante the fundamental truths at the heart of existence. As a rule these truths are known to man through Revelation as it is clarified and interpreted for his understanding by theological doctrine. Consequently, the tone of *Paradiso* is strongly doctrinal. Now to understand doctrine may require no more than the intellectual operation of the mind. But to know doctrinal truths as living realities - to know them with one's heart and soul as well as with one's mind - this kind of knowledge requires a vision which is no longer exclusively intellectual, but mystical. Since it is precisely this total experience of revealed truth that Dante wishes to convey, his progress through Paradise is set in terms of a mystic vision which illuminates and gives life to the doctrinal discussions *Paradiso* contains.

Paradiso, then, is not a course in theology, however much it may be concerned with doctrine. At the core we still find Dante's experience, which is now mystical in nature. The key which opens that experience to us and makes us share in it is his masterly use of the **imagery** of light. Dante's vision remains intensely visual, but what he now sees is the ever-increasing brilliance of light as he moves ever closer to God's throne. It was the sight of the sun which prompted his first efforts to extricate himself from the valley outside of Hell. It was the sight of the stars shining in the sky which restored him to the beauties of the world when he emerged from Hell. It was by the light of the sun that he climbed Mount Purgatory; at night it was the light of the stars which held out the promise of Paradise. That promise is fulfilled in *Paradiso* when, at the end of his journey, he is able to look into the heart of the mystery and experience the full power of the force which, as he says, moves the sun and the other stars.

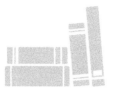

PARADISO

. . . .

CANTO 1

At the beginning of *Paradiso* Dante announces the subject of this third and last section of his **epic**: his ascent, through the heavens to God. The glory of the Mover of all things, he declares, penetrates the universe, but it shines more brightly in one part and less in another. He, Dante, has been in the heaven which most receives God's light, and there man's intellect delves so deeply that memory cannot altogether follow the experience. Still, he adds, he will relate as much as he can of that experience, and he calls on Apollo to aid him in his undertaking.

It is noon in Purgatory, and Dante, seeing Beatrice gaze at the sun, imitates her. The dazzling light is more than his eyes can sustain for long, however, and he turns once again to Beatrice, in whose eyes he sees that light reflected. Still gazing on her, he feels a change within himself, so that he no longer knows if he is still in the flesh. Without his knowing it, he and Beatrice pass through the region of fire, and Dante hears the harmony of the heavenly spheres. As he is still confused, Beatrice informs him that he has left the earth. He now wonders how he can rise against the pull of gravity, and Beatrice explains the principle of ascent in Paradise by explaining the law which regulates the movement of all created things. All things, she tells Dante move to their proper resting place according to an order established by God. It is in that orderly movement that the universe finds its resemblance to its Maker. He, the Creator, she continues, is the goal of Creation; but not all things reach him in the same sense and in the same measure. As far as man is concerned, his appointed resting place is with God in the Empyrean. It is therefore natural that he should automatically rise thither once his soul has been cleansed of all impediments; if anything, the wonder would be if he did not so rise.

Comment

The sun is the traditional symbol for God, and it is therefore altogether appropriate that here, at the beginning of his ascent through the heavens, Dante should call on Apollo for aid. In *Inferno* and *Purgatorio* Dante had invoked the Muses, the handmaidens of Apollo. Here it is the god of the sun and of poetry to whom he directs his appeal. He needs Apollo's help all the more since, as he declares, he cannot depend on his memory; the force of inspiration must come directly from God if he is to have the strength to report what he has seen.

Dante rises to the several heavens of Paradise on the strength of his desire - i.e., his love. It is, of course, divine love which makes him rise, but the magnetism of this love is transmitted to him through Beatrice. Dante thus never loses sight of the personal nature of his experience: It was the sight of her beauty which first evoked love in him; and now, in Paradise, it is still she who is at the center of his psychic experience. And the nature of Beatrice's role in Dante's life is further revealed by the fact that she grows more beautiful as they move closer to God - through her beauty God has made his beauty known to Dante and has drawn the poet to Himself.

CANTO 2

As Beatrice once again gazes at the sun and Dante looks into her eyes, they reach the first heaven, that of the Moon. Dante is surprised to find that they have entered the moon without cleaving it. The sight of this phenomenon holds out the promise that he will ultimately see the mystery held as axiomatic truth by Christians - the penetration of the divine essence into humanity in the mystery of the Incarnation. Dante then asks Beatrice about the dark shadows on the moon, shadows which he thinks are due to areas of lesser density than the bulk of the planet's substance.

Dante's question launches Beatrice into an involved scientific explanation. First, she denies any difference in the density of the moon's substance, and proceeds to demonstrate her point. If, she says, there were areas of lesser density, and if these areas ran through the entire body of the moon, then these areas would permit some sunlight to pass during an eclipse, and such is not the case. If, on the other hand, these areas do not run through the entire depth of the moon, then the denser substance behind them would reflect as much light as the surface of other areas, and there would be no shadows. (To confirm her point, Beatrice suggests to Dante that he perform an experiment: Let him place three mirrors in front of him, putting one further back than the other two, and let him then shine a light on them from behind him. All three mirrors will reflect the same brilliance, although the one further away will show a smaller image). The explanation for the shadows on the moon, Beatrice concludes, lies elsewhere.

The answer to his question, Beatrice tells Dante, is to be found in the organizing principle of the universe; the uneven brilliance of the moon is due to the same factor which causes the stars to shine with differing intensities. The undivided power of God is transmitted to the heavens below by the Primum Mobile, from which all heavenly bodies takes their brilliance and "virtue." The Primum Mobile is the heaven which gives life to the universe by giving it movement; transmitting the creative power of God, it contains implicitly the being of everything that exists. This life-giving force or spirit is then divided among various essences in the Stellar Heaven; the stars modify the original brilliance transmitted by the Primum Mobile in accordance with their specific natures and therefore shine with differing intensities. In the same way, Beatrice continues, the other heavenly bodies have differing virtues or qualities assigned to them and transmute the creative power of God in accordance with those qualities. In other words, the heavens are actually alloys between that creative power and the specific angelic intelligences which guide them; their specific brilliance is thus the result of the mingled virtue of God's spirit and their particular quality. Similarly, the moon, being uneven in quality (it is the realm of the Inconstant), shines unevenly.

Comment

Dante's argument in this canto is difficult for the modern reader, and the whole question seems altogether trivial. The question of the shadows on the moon does, however, afford him the opportunity to explain in detail the spiritual nature of the physical cosmos. Essentially, his point is that the unity that is God produces the multiplicity of created things through a process of differentiation, but that His creative power is present and active in all things, no matter how different they may seem from one another. What is especially important is that the differences are due to spiritual, not material, causes.

CANTO 3

Dante is about to tell Beatrice he has understood her lesson, when he sees faint outlines of human features. Thinking that these are reflections in a mirror, he turns around to look behind him but sees nothing. Beatrice smiles at his error as she tells him that what he has seen are the actual spirits who are placed in the moon because they have failed their vows. He thereupon speaks to one soul, who turns out to be Piccarda Donati, his friend Forese's sister (see *Purgatorio*, Cantos 23 and 24). She informs Dante of the fact that the lowest heaven is assigned to those who did not fully live up to their vows. Upon being asked whether they do not long for a higher place in Heaven, she replies that their will is in accord with the will of God, as each soul in Heaven rejoices in the order of which it is a part. The quality of love stills their will, she tells Dante; they cannot therefore desire anything but what God ordains. To desire a higher place would violate the law of love, and therefore the harmony of heaven which is the source of their joy.

Piccarda then relates something of her life. She had joined the order founded by St. Clare, but was abducted from the convent and thrown into a life which she will not describe. She points out another soul who has had a similar experience: She is Constance, who was taken from the cloister and married to Henry VI, to whom she bore Frederick II. Singing the Ave Maria, Piccarda disappears from view, and Dante turns his eyes once more to Beatrice.

Comment

Piccarda's words to Dante, "in His will is our peace," provide the key to the state of blessedness found in Paradise. Her experience thus contrasts markedly with that of Francesca, who was also forced into an unhappy marriage (see *Inferno*, Canto 5, Comment). It also contrasts with that of Pia (see *Purgatorio*, Canto 5, Comment).

CANTO 4

Two problems perplex Dante's mind after Piccarda's disappearance. He will not voice his questions, but Beatrice reads them in his countenance. First he wonders why one should be held responsible for acts in which one does not willingly participate, acts which are forced on one by another's violence. Secondly, he wonders if the appearance of the inconstant souls in the moon does not confirm Plato's doctrine, according to which souls descend into human bodies from the planets with which they are temperamentally in harmony and to which they return after death. Beatrice undertakes to tackle the second problem first. She explains that all the souls in Heaven have their permanent abode with God and his angels in the Empyrean. Their meeting places with Dante in the several heavens are merely symbolic expressions of the relative state of their spiritual blessedness; only in this manner can Dante receive the sense - impressions which, conveyed to his intellect, will inform his understanding. Plato, she concludes, was therefore wrong in suggesting that souls originate in the planets and return there after death. She adds, however, that there may be a part of truth in his words if, as some would have it, he merely meant that the praise or blame for the heavenly influences that act on men's dispositions is to be rendered to the planets rather than to men's will. It is the misunderstanding of this principle which gave rise to idolatry, causing men to worship Jupiter, Mercury, or Mars instead of God.

The other difficulty is more easily resolved, Beatrice tells Dante. The answer hinges on the distinction between free and enforced action. In the former, the will participates actively. In the latter, the will may consent passively in what is being forced on it; it may be said to participate insofar as it does nothing to oppose the enforced action. Such was the case with Piccarda and Constance, each of whom had the power to return to the cloister; if their will had remained perfect, it would have thrust them back to the life of their vows. And even though Piccarda has asserted that Constance remained faithful in her heart - a statement of the truth since souls in Paradise cannot lie, she did not keep faith in her actions.

Hearing these explanations. Dante expresses his gratitude to Beatrice. But he also sees that man's intellect can never be stated in its thirst for knowledge until it comes to rest in the all-embracing truth that is God. Until that consummation, however, each newly learned answer only raises further questions. He therefore asks Beatrice if there is any way of lessening the burden of broken vows. Beatrice's eyes now sparkle with so much love that Dante, unable to sustain the sight, is forced to look away.

Comment

Beatrice's discussion is directed against those who would deny the human will its freedom by making it the mechanical slave of outside influences, be they planetary or human. To make the moral will a slave of the individual's nature - a nature which is partly conditioned by the influence of the heavens (we would say heredity and environment) - is to deny free will. Such a denial not only robs man of moral responsibility and spiritual excellence, it makes a mockery of God's whole order by reducing it to the level of a mechanically deterministic universe. The glory of man resides in the freedom of his will; that will, Beatrice insists, cannot be coerced. Violence from the outside may make it falter; it cannot destroy its autonomy. That is why Piccarda and Constance share in the responsibility of breaking their vows.

PARADISO

CANTOS 5-9

. . . .

CANTO 5

Beatrice, delighted with Dante's progress, proceeds to answer his last question. God's greatest gift to man was freedom of the will. It follows that man's greatest gift to God is a vow, freely offered to God, since in the vow the free will sacrifices itself by its own free act. Therefore there can be no substitute for a broken vow. Yet the Church does sometimes release men from their vows. This action is to be explained by distinguishing between the content of the vow and the act of vowing itself. Nothing can annul the vow itself; only the content of the vow, the "thing offered" in the vow, may be changed with permission of the proper ecclesiastical authority. Even then, the substituted content must be greater in value than what was originally vowed. Consequently, where the original vow was of such value as to outweigh all other possible undertakings (the total dedication of self promised by monastic vows, for instance), no dispensation or substitution is possible. Mortals, Beatrice continues, must therefore never make vows lightly; and if their vow is evil, they had better break it than compound the crime by keeping it. In conclusion Beatrice admonishes Christians to be slow in making promises, and to rely on the Bible and the Church for guidance.

Having concluded her disquisition, Beatrice turns her eyes towards Heaven, and she and Dante rise to the second heaven, Mercury, which grows brighter at their presence. Lost to view in the sun's rays, Mercury is the planet where the ambitious souls who sought honor through an active life manifest themselves to Dante. These spirits appear as so many glowing lights that rush toward Dante and Beatrice, rejoicing in the presence of fresh objects of love among them. One of them, congratulating Dante on the privilege granted him of rising to God's throne while still in the flesh, offers to answer any of his questions. Encouraged by Beatrice, Dante asks him who he is and why he has been assigned to Mercury. The spirit so glows with joy at the question that his outward form is completely hidden by the brilliance of the light.

CANTO 6

The speaker is the soul of the Emperor Justinian (527–565), who organized and simplified Roman law into the code that bears his name. He begins by telling how Constantine, moving the seat of the Empire from Rome to Byzantium, reversed the progress of Aeneas from Troy to Rome. He, coming some two hundred years after Constantine, codified Roman law under the inspiration of the Holy Spirit, but only after he had come to accept the human as well as the divine nature of Christ.

Having answered Dante's question, Justinian proceeds to trace the history of the Roman Empire from its beginning with

Aeneas' arrival in Italy to its medieval form as the Holy Roman Empire. The purpose of his recital is to show the true nature of the Empire, so that Dante may see how both its usurper and its foe misconstrue it. That the Empire is worthy of reverence, Justinian declares, is shown from the very start by the sacrifice of Pallas, the Etruscan volunteer who died fighting for Aeneas' cause. Quickly passing over the founding of Trojan power in Rome some three hundred years after Aeneas' landing in Italy, and after a brief reference to the early kingdom, Justinian comes to the Republic and mentions several exemplars of civic devotion and patriotic self-sacrifice. The **climax** is reached with the founding of the Empire, first under Caesar and then under Augustus, "when all heaven willed to bring the world to its own serene mood." But these accomplishments seem small when set against the privilege granted Tiberius, the successor of Augustus, of wreaking vengeance for the Fall through the Crucifixion. And the drama was completed under Titus, when the fall of Jerusalem avenged the vengeance on the ancient sin. The Empire's further justification, Justinian concludes, may be found in the fact that under Charlemagne the Holy Roman Empire defended the Church against the attacks of the Lombards of Northern Italy.

Now that Dante has seen the history of the Empire, Justinian tells him, he can judge for himself the actions of the Guelfs and the Ghibellines, the former opposing it with the help of France, the others reducing it to a mere adjunct in a factional struggle.

Turning his attention to the second part of Dante's initial question, Justinian now explains that the second heaven contains the souls of those who strove for honor and fame; their virtue was tainted somewhat by ambition and anxiety for worldly re-nown. They are now free from envious desire, however, and they rejoice in the heavenly harmony of which they are a part.

As if to demonstrate his point that greatness and smallness are harmonized, he points out Romeo of Villeneuve, minister to the Count of Provence, who was maligned to his master despite his honest management of the Count's affairs, and who resigned his office to return to a life of poverty in his old age.

Comment

Justinian's speech is the heavenly justification of Empire as the institution designed for the temporal rule of mankind. The fact that Justinian, the codifier of Roman law, is the speaker, indicates once again that Dante's conception of the Empire was utopian - it was the ideal of universal peace under law which appealed to him. But universal peach under law may be a purely secular ideal; for Dante, as for the prophets of the Old Testament, it was an integral part of God's plan for mankind. For at the center of Dante's justification of the Empire stands the Christian Redemption, and Justinian's rehearsal of Roman history is designed only to show that everything in history was a preparation for that central act on which the salvation of mankind depends. Political and religious history meet in the Crucifixion: Not only does God's sanctioning of the Empire appear in the fact that Christ chose to be born under Augustus, but the Empire is made the instrument of God's punishment for original sin. And finally, it was the Empire, under Titus, which punished the sin of slaying Christ by capturing Jerusalem.

Church and Empire, Dante asserts over and over again, are interdependent. The codification of Roman law was inspired by the Holy Spirit, but the inspiration could come only after Justinian was converted to the orthodox doctrine of the double nature of Christ, human as well as divine. Dante insists on this detail because the purpose of law is to regulate human life, and only after he accepts Christ's humanity can Justinian undertake the task of regulating human conduct. But if the task of the Empire must rest on orthodox doctrine, the work of the Church is equally dependent on the presence of the Empire: It is the Empire which fostered the growth of the Church (thereby fostering the spread of Christianity and its fruits), and it is the Empire which is the natural champion of the Church against political and factional encroachment.

CANTO 7

Justinian sings a brief hymn of triumph; then he and the other spirits vanish from sight as they resume their dance. Dante is now beset with another question, and Beatrice, reading his thought, proceeds to answer it. The problem that vexes him is how a just vengeance - the expiation of original sin on the Cross - can be justly punished. (In other words, if the Crucifixion was an act of divine justice, how can it have deserved punishment?) In order to answer this question, Beatrice explains the Fall and the Redemption.

The Fall, Beatrice tells Dante, was due to Adam's inability to control his will. Because of that failure, human nature, created pure and in harmony with its Maker, became contaminated. By that one act the entire human race was lost. In order to redeem mankind the Word of God descended and, in an act of love, united to Himself, in His own person, the now sullied human nature. That human nature suffered on the Cross the just punishment for its sin; insofar as Christ was human his expiation of original sin satisfied the demands of divine justice. But Christ is also the manifestation of God as the Son, and insofar as he is divine, the Crucifixion was an outrage to his divinity. At the act of justice God rejoiced and heaven opened. But, Beatrice concludes, the Jews exulted at the outrage, and the earth trembled; for this sacrilege they had to be punished, and consequently Jerusalem fell.

Beatrice's explanation only raises another question in Dante's mind; why did God will this particular method of redemption? The answer, Beatrice tells him, can be understood only by those whose intellect has been "matured" in the flame of love. Divine Goodness, she explains, has created men and angels out of Itself to display Its eternal beauty. Whatever God has created without intermediary is immortal and free, bearing the stamp of its divine origin; it is not subject to the changing influence of the heavens. Such was man until sin made him fall from his God-like state and thus lose his resemblance to his Creator. Having lost his privileged position through his own fault, man could regain it in only one of two ways: Either God could forgive him and remit his sin, or man could offer satisfaction for his fault. To offer satisfaction, however, man's atonement must somehow equal the gravity of the sin. As man cannot possible lower himself beneath his station to the same degree that he tried to rise above it when he ate the forbidden fruit, this solution was out of question. Therefore God had to reinstate man. But, wishing man to participate in some measure in the Redemption. He joined justice to mercy. By means of the Incarnation He combined the two ways: The Son's offer of himself was a gift of love, and his suffering as man afforded human nature the opportunity to atone for its sin.

But Dante has yet another question for Beatrice. The elements and their combinations are also part of Creation, and yet they are subject to corruption and dissolution. How can that be, if all Creation is immortal like its Creator? The angels and the heavens, Beatrice replies, were created directly by God, as was the prime matter out of which the elements and their compounds are formed. But these latter, as well as the animals and plants derived from them, were formed by the creative "virtue" possessed by the angels, the stars, and the planetary heavens; hence they are not immortal. Man, on the other hand, was also the direct creation of God; and, Beatrice concludes, Dante may infer the resurrection of the body from this fact, since God created man's body as well as his soul.

Comment

In connection with Justinian's discussion of Empire, Beatrice is led to discourse on the Redemption, the central **theme** of *Paradiso*. At first glance her speech may appear terribly pedantic, but it is more than an academic discussion of a difficult point. To understand Redemption, one must understand man's position in relation to his Maker, and it is this position that Beatrice seeks to define for Dante. Once again the author of *the Divine Comedy* insists on the dignity conferred upon man by the act of Creation - man is an autonomous being enjoying complete freedom in, and responsibility for, his actions. What links him to God is love, a free gift of the spirit, and not the determinism of a mechanistic universe. Hence Beatrice underscores the fact that man, like the angels, is a direct creation of God.

The important point is that man is not a slave; neither God nor planetary influences control his will. He is, it is true, dependent on God, but this dependency takes the form of the mutual bond of freely given love. It is indeed God's love that saves mankind. But the redemption would be meaningless if man were not allowed to participate in it by joining his will and love to the will and love of God. If God were simply to forgive man's transgressions and let it go at that, then man would be reduced to the level of an irresponsible animal, a toy in the hands of a benign deity. It is not God's harshness, but man's self-respect as an individual which demands human participation in the act of redemption. Redemption is a cooperative venture; alone, man cannot accomplish it, but if his freedom is to have any meaning he must willingly share in the undertaking. The incarnation of Christ in man was the means that achieved this end.

CANTO 8

Seeing Beatrice grow more beautiful, Dante knows they have risen to the third heaven, Venus. The amorous spirits manifested there leave their cosmic dance to greet the poet, and one of them declares that they wish to be of service to the man who once addressed a poem to them. (The poem is Dante's ode, "You who by understanding move the third heaven.") Asked to identify himself, the spirit says that it is the glow of his joy which keeps Dante from recognizing him; he is Dante's princely friend, Charles Martel, son of Charles II of Apulia and grandson of Charles of Anjou. King of Hungary, and heir to the County of Provence and the Kingdom of Naples. He states that much of the evil that is to befall Italy would not have happened had he lived longer. Dante is overjoyed at seeing his friend, and, he tells Charles, his joy is increased by his knowledge that his friend perceives it, and by the further thought that it is perceived through God. As Charles had briefly criticized his brother Robert for his degeneracy, Dante asks how it is that degenerate children are born to noble parents. His friend explains that the diversity of gifts required by human society is provided for by the action of the heavens on human nature, and the celestial influence overrules natural heredity. Thus not everyone is necessarily suited for the position into which he is born. If the world were to assign men their places in accordance with their natural gifts instead of looking to heredity or other irrelevant considerations, much confusion would be avoided.

PARADISO

PARADISO: CANTOS 9–20

CANTO 9

Charles turns again to God, and his place is taken by Cunizza, sister of the hated tyrant, Ezzelino da Romano, and noted for her amours while on earth. She is in the third heaven, she tells Dante, because of her earthly loves, but her past sins no longer trouble her. She points out the troubadour Folco whose fame, she declares, will long endure; and she bewails the fact that her countrymen no longer seek such fame. Denouncing their crimes and predicting endless woe for them, she returns to the cosmic dance.

Dante now directs his attention to Folco, whose appearance glows more brightly. Since God sees all, and Folco sees all through God, why, asks Dante, does he delay so long in answering his unspoken question? For his part, Dante would not wait this long were he in Folco as Folco is in him. In reply the troubadour speaks of his birthplace, Marseilles, and of his amorous youth.

He explains to Dante that there is no repentance in heaven (a question undoubtedly raised in Dante's mind by Cunizza's statement) because the sin is remembered only as the occasion of God's power to redeem. He then points out the light that is the spirit of Rahab (the harlot who helped Joshua take Jericho), and mentions the fact that the third heaven falls just within the range of the earth's shadow, a fact which accounts for her presence in it. He then refers to Rahab's help in the conquest of the Holy Land and denounces the Pope's indifference to its recovery. It is Florence, he concludes, the city planted by the devil himself, that corrupts the world with its accursed flower (the gold florin, from "fiorino," meaning "little flower"). Its gold has turned the shepherd to a wolf, and Pope and Cardinals give no thought to the Gospels or to Nazareth. But retribution, he proclaims, will soon overtake them.

Comment

In the third heaven, the heaven of love, the principle of the spiritual companionship of the blessed in God is established. It is by virtue of that spiritual identity that Dante rejoices in his friend Charles' knowledge of his feelings through God; it is also by virtue of that identity that Cunizza and Folco can answer his questions without his having to ask them.

Folco of Marseilles was a troubadour poet who later became a Cisterian monk; as bishop of Toulouse, he took a leading part in the Albigensian Crusade directed against the Catharist heresy which flourished in southern France. He appears here as the exemplar of a nature dedicated to love, which, under the discipline of a religious life, learned to direct its passion to God.

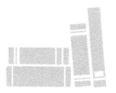

PARADISO

CANTOS 10–15

CANTO 10

Dante opens this canto with a statement about the process of Creation as it operates in the Trinity. The Father, gazing upon the Son with the Love which eternally emanates from both, created the universe of sense and intellect; the order of that universe reveals God to those who contemplate it. Dante then proceeds to a discussion of the providential way in which the sun was placed to insure the generation of life on earth. After this introduction, Dante tells us that Beatrice's increased beauty, reflecting the light of the sun informs him that they have risen to the fourth heaven. It is the circle of the Sun, the realm of the Prudent or Wise, where the masters of theology enjoy their state of blessedness by contemplating how God "breathes and begets." Beatrice urges Dante to give thanks to the "sun of the angels" for having raised him to the sphere of the sensible sun, and for a moment Dante is so absorbed by his love for God that he forgets the beauty of his lady. Her pleasure at the intensity of his spiritual experience expresses itself in a smile so beautiful that it quite shatters the single-minded concentration of his spirit and draws him back to the many objects that surround him.

Twelve blazing spirits now surround Dante and Beatrice, forming a circle which Dante likens to a crown of stars. Singing songs of such unutterable beauty as cannot even be imagined on earth, they dance round the pair three times, and then pause, as if waiting for the music to resume. A voice from among them declares that divine grace, which kindles true love, has so touched Dante's soul as to lead him up the stairway to heaven.

It would be as unnatural for them to refuse any request of his as for water not to flow down to the sea. He therefore responds to Dante's unspoken wish by identifying the spirits who form the circle. He is Thomas Aquinas, he tells Dante, and he proceeds to name the eleven other spirits, who represent a variety of approaches to wisdom and truth. After he has completed his enumeration, the "glorious wheel" begins to revolve once more to the accompaniment of ineffable music.

CANTO 11

The glorious harmony of the dance and music leads Dante to contemplate, for a moment, the nature of earthly existence, where men devote their energy to the pursuit of so many illusory satisfactions, while he, released from the turmoil of earthly concerns, is so gloriously received in heaven. When the dance stops, St. Thomas speaks to him once more. Providence, he tells Dante, raised two Princes to guide the Church in her path towards God. One, St. Francis of Assisi, followed the path of love; the other, St. Dominic, pursued the road of wisdom. Aquinas says he will speak of St. Francis.

Francis, St. Thomas declares, rose from Assisi as the sun rises in the East. Rejecting his earthly inheritance, he publicly espoused Poverty, and the ardor of his love brought him many disciples, all pledged to Poverty. As the number of his disciples grew, he founded his order, which was twice confirmed by two Popes. He tried to convert the Egyptians, and preached before the Sultan. He received the stigmata (the impress of nails and lance as a sign of oneness of spirit with Christ) and bore their mark for two years. When he died, he commended his Lady Poverty to his brethren, bidding them to love her faithfully. If St. Francis was such, Aquinas concludes, only think what Dominic must have been to be a worthy colleague of his in the guidance of the Church! But, he adds, the Dominicans have now almost all grown degenerate.

CANTO 12

As soon as St. Thomas has finished speaking, the "sacred millstone" begins to revolve once more. Before its first revolution is completed, a second circle of lights surrounds it and accords its movement and song to the dance and music of the first. When the two circles come to a rest, a voice from the second ring addresses Dante. It is Bonaventura, the Franciscan, who undertakes to praise St. Dominic just as Thomas, the Dominican, has praised St. Francis. Where one is praised, says Bonaventura, the other must be praised too, for they fought in the same cause and their glory must shine in union.

Dominic was born in Spain, Bonaventura tells Dante, and even before his birth, his calling was foreshadowed by a dream that came to his mother. He followed the counsel of Christ and embraced poverty, but his true glory consisted in his zeal for the faith. He became a great teacher. Scorning ecclesiastical benefice, he demanded the right to found his order to combat heresy. He devoted his learning and energy to that task, and from him sprang many streams which irrigate the "Catholic orchard." If, concludes Bonaventura, such was one wheel of the chariot wherein the Church defended herself, the excellence of that other, whose praise was spoken by St. Thomas, should be clear enough. But the Franciscans are ruined nowadays by the division in their order, as they fight over the strictness and laxity of observance of the rules. By way of closing Bonaventura then names himself and the others who form the second circle of lights.

CANTO 13

Let the reader, says Dante, imagine the twenty-four brightest stars in the sky (and here Dante names specific stars and constellations) arranged into two crowns, and he will have a dim shadow of the two circles that sweep around him and Beatrice. The spirits sing of the three Persons in the one nature of God, and of the two natures in the one Person of Christ. The two circles having come to a pause, St. Thomas speaks once more. His passing remark, in Canto 10, that none ever rose to equal Solomon in wisdom has perplexed Dante, and the saint undertakes to explain himself.

The question about Solomon's wisdom becomes the starting point of a discourse on the whole range of Creation, with its beginning in the Trinity. All things mortal and immortal are nothing but reflections of the Divine Idea which emanates from the Father as an act of love. The living Light - which emanates from the Father without departing from Him or from the Love which is the third Person of the Trinity - that Light is broken into the manifestations of the nine heavens while remaining one within itself. It is refracted through these heavens onto all created things, giving form to the prime matter out of which the physical universe is built. However, both the imprinting influences of heaven and the receptivity of matter to the imprints are not always equally propitious, and this fact accounts for differences in excellence in the world. Nonetheless, matter was perfectly disposed in its receptivity and the imprinting power of heaven was at its highest when Adam was created and Christ was conceived. Dante, therefore, is right in supposing that Adam and Christ possessed all human knowledge in perfection.

If this assertion seems to contradict the earlier statement about Solomon's wisdom, the contradiction, St. Thomas continues, is easily resolved. For Solomon did not ask for all knowledge; he merely desired the wisdom necessary to be a good king. Furthermore, Thomas had declared that none ever rose to equal Solomon's wisdom, and the use of the word shows that it applies only to kings, of whom there are many, but few good ones. The contradiction is thus resolved, and St. Thomas cautions Dante against jumping to rash conclusions through failure to make necessary distinctions. For once we form a biased opinion, vanity prevents us from seeing the truth. To set out fishing for the truth without the proper skill is far worse than not seeking after truth altogether. Both philosophy and theology present many sad examples of falsehood mistaken for truth. And seemingly obvious moral judgments may be as rash and false as intellectual ones.

CANTO 14

St. Thomas having concluded, Beatrice voices the yet unformed thought of Dante: Will the resurrection of the body not reimpose limitations on the now emancipated souls in heaven? The spirits now break into a hymn; three times they sing the mystery of the Trinity - "That One and Two and Three who ever liveth and reigneth ever in Three and Two and One, not circumscribed, but circumscribing all." Then Solomon proceeds to answer Beatrice's question.

Human nature, Solomon explains, includes both body and soul; the disembodied soul is, therefore, less complete than the whole person. When, at the time of the resurrection, the glorified flesh will be resumed by the soul, the person shall be complete once more. Being complete, the person will be more pleasing to God, and will therefore receive more of his light. The fully resurrected person will thus see God more clearly and therefore love Him all the more and experience an increase of joy. And the organs of sense will be strong enough to sustain that glory and take pleasure in it.

A resounding Amen, shouted by the other spirits, greets the end of Solomon's discourse. This cry indicates to Dante their desire to be reunited with their bodies. At this point a third circle of lights appears, at first faintly, then in a sudden flash which nearly blinds Dante. He turns to Beatrice, the beauty of whose smile makes him quite forget what he has seen, and instantaneously he finds himself in the fifth heaven, Mars. Filled with gratitude at this latest sign of divine grace, he offers a silent prayer of thanks to God; the dazzling radiance which shines forth from the planet tells him his prayer has been accepted before it has even left his heart. Overwhelmed by the brilliance of the light which sparkles from the glowing planet, Dante cries out to God his wonderment.

The spirits of the warriors, so many shining sparks of light, form a brightly shining cross against the red glow of the planet. The cross flashes forth Christ, Dante tells us, and he begs the reader's forgiveness for his inability to describe the sight. He sees lights moving back and forth along the limbs of the cross, and from these lights there comes a melody, in the form of hymns of victory which he can only partly understand, a melody whose beauty surpasses anything he has experienced thus far. And he hastens to explain that he means no slight to Beatrice's beauty by this remark, for he has not yet looked upon her in this heaven.

Comment

The cantos devoted to the realm of the Sun are among the most difficult to be found in *Paradiso*. They deal with wisdom - i.e., knowledge and the proper application of that knowledge. In other words, Dante's subject here is the search for truth. Since truth is divine in origin, it is one and indivisible, just as God's spirit is one and indivisible. But just as the oneness of God's spirit is split up among the several parts of the created universe which reflect whatever light shines on them (see St. Thomas's discourse, Canto 13), so truth, as it is manifested in the world, has many facets. It follows that there are, in the world, different kinds of knowledge suited to different types of interest and human activity. Consequently Dante places in the two wheeling circles kings, lawyers, grammarians, mystics, as well as philosophers and theologians. And to show the complementary nature of the various kinds of knowledge, he has them dance and sing as a unit, for all knowledge is unified in God.

As all spiritual things tend to return to their source, so wisdom ultimately turns to God. But even here the ways of approaching the Supreme Being may differ. That difference is illustrated by the complementary lives of St. Francis and St. Dominic, the former knowing and serving God through love, the latter through intellectual wisdom. For that matter, both ways are not only equally valid, but equally needed for the well-being of the Church, which is the repository of God's word and its interpreter: Both St. Thomas (Canto 11) and St. Bonaventura (Canto 12) assert that to praise one is automatically to praise the other.

The business of St. Francis and St. Dominic was with spiritual affairs. But human life is not exclusively spiritual; it is social and political as well. Temporal affairs are the province of kings and rulers, and that is why Dante introduces St. Thomas's brief praise of Solomon, the king who sought the wisdom to be a just ruler (Canto 13). The point is unmistakably clear: Only Adam and Christ possessed perfect human knowledge; all other knowledge is partial, and Solomon chose the kind of knowledge appropriate to his calling. And since knowledge on earth tends to be fragmentary, Aquinas cautions Dante against hasty conclusions in the search for truth.

Solomon appears as the example of the perfect temporal ruler, who must minister to the needs of the complete human personality - body and soul. It is therefore fitting that the task of explaining the resurrection of the body should be assigned to him, since he, better than the others, understands the complete person in which flesh and spirit are joined. God's supreme gift to man is his identity as a free, distinct individual; his freedom is spiritual, but his identity as an individual is conferred on him and defined by his body. Man will attain the perfection of his being - as Adam and Christ were perfect - only when his fleshly garb is restored to him; then, retaining for all time his perfect individuality, his love for his Maker will increase.

The wedding of the spirit to the flesh is a mystery of Creation, stemming from Divine Love. It is most radiantly manifested in the dual nature of Christ, which the wheeling circles celebrate before St. Thomas explains his praise of Solomon (Canto 13). But Creation itself is a mystery, a mystery contained in the Holy Trinity. Therefore, to understand human destiny one must eventually seek to understand the nature of God. In other words, all human knowledge finds its ultimate fulfillment in knowledge of God. In the first three heavens of Paradise, Dante was concerned with establishing the nature of man's freedom in relation to his Maker. Here, in the realm of the Sun - itself a symbol of God, he undertakes the almost superhuman task of defining the nature of the deity in relation to the universe. That **theme** is clearly announced when Dante first enters the realm of the Sun: At the opening of the tenth canto a brief statement defines the self-contained yet creative nature of the Holy Trinity. It is picked up in the thirteenth canto, where the emotional impact of the mystery is expressed in the song of the two wheeling circles, and where it is defined intellectually in St. Thomas' discourse on Creation. And it is sounded once again in the fourteenth canto, in the hymn about the nature of the Trinity which precedes Solomon's discussion of the resurrection of the body.

The mystery of the Holy Trinity is not solved in the realm of the Sun; the complete vision of its nature is attainable only in the Empyrean, where all knowledge is one. Yet it is symbolically present in the image of the double crown of wheeling circles, an image which is completed with the appearance of that third circle, symbolic of the Holy Spirit the inspiring, creative force of Love. Only through such symbols can the Divine Nature be apprehended, and at this stage of his journey, the sight is more than Dante's being can sustain. The third crown is a **foreshadowing** of the final vision in the Empyrean. But Dante is not yet ready for it, and he instinctively returns his gaze to Beatrice.

CANTO 15

The hymns of the warriors of God cease, and one of the spirits shoots like a falling star to the foot of the cross to greet Dante, whom he calls his descendant. He speaks of his eager longing for Dante's arrival, and bids Dante speak out his questions even though they are known to him. Dante asks for his name, but the spirit at first merely identifies himself as Dante's great-great-grandfather. He then speaks of Florence as it was in the olden days, when it abode in peace - sober and chaste. He briefly describes the simple life of its citizens, untroubled by discordant ambitions. There he was born, baptized (here he gives his name, Cacciaguida), and married. He was knighted by the emperor Conrad III, whom he followed in his crusade of 1147. It was on that crusade that he died in battle and rose to the peace of heaven.

PARADISO

CANTO 16-20

· ·

CANTO 16

Proud of his ancestor's nobility, Dante now addresses him ceremoniously, whereupon Beatrice smiles warningly at his rising vanity. He then questions Cacciaguida about his ancestry, his birth, and the noble families of ancient Florence. In reply Cacciaguida tells him the date of his birth (1091) and the place where his ancestors lived; he declines to speak of their identity or origin. He then turns his attention to Florence, the population of which, he says, was one-fifth of what it is today. Furthermore, its citizenry was pure; it had not been adulterated by the influx from neighboring regions. But the undue growth of Florence brought in its wake the lust for power and factional divisions which have corrupted the civic life. There follows a dirge on the great families of Florence, and Cacciaguida concludes by bemoaning the broken troth which set two families, the Amidei and the Buondelmonti, against each other.

CANTO 17

Encouraged by Beatrice, Dante now asks Cacciaguida to explain the various hints about his future that he has heard along his journey, and Cacciaguida tells him in plain language what is in store for him. At the instigation of the Pope, he will be falsely accused by his native city and banished. Slandered, exiled, he will know the pain of leaving all that is dear to him. He will also taste the bitterness of having to depend on the bounty of strangers. But the worst he will have to suffer will be his isolation; for the evil ways of his companions in exile will cause him to sever all contact with them, and he will form a party of one.

His first refuge, Cacciaguida continues, will be with Bartolomeo della Scala, Lord of Verona, who will anticipate all his requests by granting them. There he will meet Bartolomeo's brother, Can Grande, who shall give signs of his worth before Henry VII descends into Italy, Dante should look to Can Grande, Cacciaguida adds, because he will bring about great changes in the world, and his deeds will be such that even those who behold them will scarcely believe them. (Dante however, does not specify the nature of those deeds, for Cacciaguida tells him to retain them in his memory but not to set them down.) Such, then, is his future, Cacciaguida concludes; yet Dante should not be envious of his neighbors, for he will by far out-live the punishment of his enemies.

Dante now asks if he should not be cautious in setting down what has been revealed to him in the course of his journey. He fears that some of the truths he has learned may be unpleasant and may earn him the enmity of those on whose protection he will have to depend. Yet he also fears that if he shrinks from telling the truth he will lose his place in the afterlife. But Cacciaguida tells him to banish all hesitancy from his mind - "make thy entire vision manifest." If the truth hurts at first, it will eventually heal the wounds it touches. In his journey through the three realms of eternal life only famous souls have been made known to him so that his report might impress the living, who would otherwise remain unimpressed by the example of obscure or unknown characters.

Comment

The cross on Mars is the symbolic expression of the kind of spiritual zeal to be found in the fifth heaven, just as the double crown of lights symbolized the specific spiritual nature of the Sun. The spirits on Mars are the soldiers of Christ (hence the cross) who, inspired by Love (the red hue of the planet) and armed with the true Faith (the white color of the cross), have gone into the world to do battle for their Lord. Their prototype is the ideal medieval knight, who owes his temporal allegiance to the emperor from whom he derives his knighthood, but who has dedicated his arms to the service of God. His mission in life is best exemplified by the crusade, since, under the banner of the Empire, he fights for the liberation of the Holy Land. His death in that cause can only be glorious.

It is altogether fitting that the subject of Dante's years of exile should come up at this point. For one thing, it offers the implied contrast between Cacciaguida's selfless dedication to an ideal and the self-centered factionalism which rends not only Florence, but the whole world. For another, it gives Dante the opportunity of voicing his high hopes for Can Grande (to whom, incidentally, he dedicated the *Paradiso*). Can Grande, he thought, might be the very man to take up the mission of the medieval knight and fight to restore a righteous order in the world. (Cacciaguida's prophecy concerning him is necessarily vague since, at the time Dante wrote, Can Grande had not yet accomplished anything remarkable.) Lastly, Dante can draw the courage he himself will need to sustain the bitterness of exile and isolation from the example of the fifth heaven.

In connection with the last point, it should be noted that Dante actually takes on the role of a warrior of God. He, too, Cacciaguida tells him, will go out into the world and single-handedly do battle for God's cause. His shield will be his righteousness, confirmed by the grace which permits him to rise to heaven before his time. And his lance will be the truth that is being revealed to him. Therefore he must banish fear and reveal all, no matter what the personal cost to himself maybe.

CANTO 18

Cacciaguida has stopped speaking, and Dante is absorbed in his own thoughts, "tempering the bitter with the sweet," as he ponders what he has heard. Beatrice's words of consolation rouse him from his meditation, only to plunge him into the equally absorbing bliss of gazing joyfully into her eyes, and she must now remind him that Paradise is not only in those eyes. She draws his attention back to Cacciaguida, who names some of the famous spirits contained in the cross. Having finished his recital, Cacciaguida returns to his place, where he joins the other spirits in their hymns.

As Dante turns once more to Beatrice, he becomes aware of her yet greater beauty, and knows, by that sign, that they have risen to a higher sphere. He looks about him and notices that the white glow of Jupiter has replaced the reddish hue of Mars. They are now in the sixth heaven, the realm of the Just. There the spirits form, in succession, the letters of the opening words of the Book of Wisdom: "Diligite justitiam, qui judicatis terram" ("Love righteousness, ye that be judges of the earth," Wisdom, i:1). The last letter being an M, other spirits join themselves to it and gradually transform it into a gigantic eagle.

The sight of that eagle (symbol of Roman law and justice) causes Dante to pray to God that He would cleanse the mercenary Church which pollutes the pure rays of Justice emanating from this planet. And he concludes with a warning to Pope John XXII, who issues excommunications only to revoke them on payment of money. But, Dante adds ironically, the Pope may yet plead as his excuse that he is totally absorbed in the contemplation of John the Baptist (whose image was stamped on the gold florin).

CANTO 19

The spirits of the just kings, who compose the eagle, speaks as one person, with one voice. Dante asks them to resolve the doubt that has beset him for many years, the nature of which, he says, they know. The eagle responds to Dante's request by affirming that God's wisdom exceeds all that the created universe expresses. The proof of this fact, it declares, is to be found in the experience of Lucifer, who stood first in the order of creation, and who fell because, unable to see all, he could not wait for the greater illumination God would have given him. If Lucifer's vision was limited, it follows that lesser natures are all the more limited in what they can see and understand. Only God can see to the depths of divine justice. Furthermore, man's very idea of justice is derived from God, and this thought alone should still any questioning of God's justice. Now Dante, the eagle says, feels it is unjust that the virtuous heathen should be excluded from Redemption; but who is he to judge? The will of God is justice, and whatever is in harmony with it is therefore just.

The eagle then reaffirms the principle that only those who believe in Christ can hope to rise to heaven. And yet, it adds, many who call upon His name will be further from Him on Judgment Day than many a heathen who does not know Him. On that day, too, the wickedness and incompetence of many contemporary kings will be disclosed. And the eagle concludes with a detailed indictment of European rulers of the day.

CANTO 20

The spirits who compose the eagle now burst into a chime of many notes. After that music has been stilled, a murmuring sound is heard which rises into a single voice once more, as the eagle resumes its discourse. It calls Dante's attention to the lights which form its eye and declares that these are its chief spirits. It proceeds to enumerate them: King David, who celebrated God in song and brought the Ark of the Covenant to Jerusalem, forms the pupil of the eye; the eyebrow is composed of the emperor Trajan, the Hebrew king Hezekiah, the emperor Constantine, William of Sicily, and the Trojan Ripheus. And the eagle underscores the fact that a Trojan is among the blessed. Dante is so amazed that he cannot help exclaim in wonder at the presence of two pagans (Trajan and Ripheus); the eagle declares that both died in the true faith. Trajan, thanks to the prayers of St. Gregory, was allowed to return to earth from Limbo long enough to be converted to Christianity; Ripheus was granted the illumination of grace before the coming of Christ so that he died believing in Christ to come. And the eagle concludes by declaring that the mystery of divine justice is not to be fathomed by man, since even the spirits who see God do not know who shall be saved. But they rejoice in this limitation of their knowledge, for it allows them the freedom to attune their will to the will of God.

Dante's vision of divine justice has now been corrected, and he rejoices at the thought that it transcends doctrinal knowledge and holds out the possibility of salvation to the truly righteous everywhere.

Comment

In the sixth heaven Dante takes up a question which has haunted men at least since the time of the Book of Job: Is God just? For Dante the question takes the specific form of wondering how a just God can condone the damnation of righteous men and women whose only crime is that they happen not to have been born Christians. The eagle's reply is that to speak of an unjust God is a contradiction in terms, since the very idea of justice stems from God. Man must learn to accept his limitations; he cannot know all. But such an answer does not satisfy man's sense of fair play, and Dante suggests that Divine Providence may yet save many who, on the basis of doctrine, would have to be rejected. Anything pertaining to God is ultimately a mystery, and it is with this sense of mystery that Dante leaves the question. The only way to make one's peace with the mystery is to accept it - consciously, deliberately, by harmonizing one's will to the will of God.

But God's justice does not manifest itself only in the mysterious operations of Divine Providence which transcend doctrinally received knowledge. In other words, divine justice does not operate only in relation to salvation; it also operates in relation to the temporal life of man. Humanity requires justice in this life as well as in the afterlife, and here God's instrument is the temporal ruler, the king. The eagle has thus a double meaning. As the bird of Jupiter, king of the classical gods of antiquity, it is the symbol of Divine Justice, which is identical with the will of God. And since God is not multiple, but one, the eagle speaks with but a single voice. But the eagle is also the traditional symbol of Empire, and as such it represents the ideal of law and order by means of which justice is dispensed to mankind. The function of Dante's ideal Empire is to bring the justice of universal law and order to the entire world. Its supreme mission is a mission of justice. This idea is indicated by the fact that the eagle takes shape around the letter M, standing for Monarchy.

Finally, the symbolism of the eagle expresses the relationship between human and divine justice. When speaking of the principle of justice the kings speaks as one, because justice is one. But as righteousness can take many forms, they sing as individuals, yet their notes form a harmony. They are in harmony because their righteousness is a reflection of divine justice, from which their justice as rulers derives. In other words, temporal rule must reflect divine justice if it is to be just. Thus the ideal Empire, by founding a peaceful order in justice, will manifest God's presence in the temporal life of the world. This idea is expressed in the choice of King David for the pupil of the eagle's eye: The great singer of man's love for God was also the man who effected the return of the Ark of the Covenant, wherein God's presence was manifested, to its rightful place among the Chosen People.

PARADISO

CANTOS 21–25

....

CANTO 21

Again, Dante turns to Beatrice, who tells him she **refrains** from smiling lest her beauty shatter his mortal senses. For they have now risen to the seventh heaven, Saturn, the heaven identified with Temperance, where the souls of the contemplative are revealed. Dante sees a golden ladder stretching up and out of sight; it is Jacob's ladder on which descend splashes of bright light. Dante asks the one that has come closest to him why the music of heaven is no longer heard, and the spirit replies that his hearing, like his sight, is that of a mortal, and therefore is not ready to bear the divine harmony sounded in Saturn. Dante has also asked why this spirit has come nearer to him than the others; the answer is that Divine Love has assigned the office of welcoming Dante to him. Dante then asks why he, and no other, was given this specific task. Before answering, the spirit whirls and glows in ecstasy at his oneness with the light of God which shines on him. He tells Dante he can see the Supreme Essence, but not even the highest of the Seraphim (the highest order of angels, closest to God) can see the answer to that question: The answer lies too deep in the very Being of God. And he bids Dante carry back to the world a warning against presuming to read with its clouded vision what the clear vision of the spirits in heaven cannot fathom.

A chastened Dante abandons the question and instead asks to know who has been speaking with him. The spirit identifies himself as Peter Damian, renowned for his ascetic life, and proceeds to denounce the pomp and luxury of present-day dignitaries of the Church. At his words a host of lights descend the ladder and, placing themselves around him, raise a thunderous cry which so stuns Dante that he cannot understand its meaning.

CANTO 22

Beatrice reassures Dante and tells him that the cry he has heard invoked divine vengeance, which, she says, will strike before he dies. The brightest among the lights that have come down the ladder now steps forward. It is St. Benedict, founder of the Benedictine order and of its first monastery at Monte Cassino. The seventh heaven, he tells Dante, contains the souls of those who, cloistered from the world, devoted themselves to a life of meditation and contemplation. Dante asks the saint if he may see his "uncovered image" - i.e., see him as he appeared in life, and Benedict replies that the wish will be granted in the last sphere, the Empyrean, where all wishes have their fulfillment. There, beyond space and time, each desire is "perfect, ripe, and whole."

It is to that realm, Benedict continues, that the golden ladder of Saturn leads. And he adds that this is the same ladder that Jacob saw in his dream, laden with angels. Now, however, no one on earth seeks to rise on it. The rules of his own order, says Benedict, are not followed. The monasteries, which were once houses of prayer, are now dens, and the hoods of the monks are so many sacks "full of foul meal." Yet usury is not nearly as offensive to God as the all - too - common practice of misusing monastic funds for private ends. And the saint goes on to deplore the weakness of mankind, which is so easily seduced that the noblest ideals quickly degenerate. Neither St. Peter, nor St. Francis, nor he himself sought money; yet if Dante will compare these beginnings with the current practice he will see how quickly white has changed to black.

Having concluded his discourse, St. Benedict rejoins the assembled lights, and all are swept in a whirlwind to the highest heaven. With a sign, Beatrice sweeps Dante up the ladder after them, and he comes to rest in the constellation of Gemini, under the sign of which he was born. Now that he has reached the eighth heaven, the sphere of the fixed stars, he is about to encounter the triumphant souls of the redeemed. But first Beatrice bids him look back over the path he has traveled. Looking down, Dante sees the seven planetary heavens, and beyond them the tiny earth, the "threshing floor that makes us so fierce." Having taken in the sight, Dante turns his eyes to those of Beatrice.

Comment

Temperance, the moral virtue associated with Saturn, was thought to mean ascetic detachment from material things for the sake of total absorption in spiritual matters. Saturn, then, is the realm of the contemplative life, the pure life of the spirit, which was rated higher than the active life because it led directly to heaven. The direct connection between contemplation and heavenly life is expressed in the symbolism of the golden ladder, which starts on Saturn and leads to the Empyrean. In heaven, just as on earth, the contemplative souls live close to God, and they manifest themselves on their planet just long enough to converse with Dante. (On the other planets the manifested souls remain after Dante's passage; here, they can hardly wait to return to God, and rise ahead of the poet.) The intensely spiritual nature of Saturn is also indicated by the silence that greets Dante on his arrival: The music is of such spiritual intensity that Dante's mortal senses are not attuned to it. Like Beatrice's beauty if she were to smile, the music would shatter his senses if he were to hear it.

Generally speaking, when the Church or the monastic orders are castigated in *the Divine Comedy*, it is for their meddling in temporal affairs. Here, however, in the sphere of spiritual contemplation, it is for their materialism, their betrayal of the spiritual ideal on which they were founded, that they are taken to task.

When the contemplative saints are swept back up to the highest heaven, Dante is thrust up the ladder after them by the spiritual action of Beatrice - i.e., by the power of Love. This imitation of the contemplative spirits' movement indicates that Dante, too, now possesses the contemplative vision needed to grasp the truths which are about to be revealed to him. If his climb up the mountain of Purgatory effected the moral purification of Dante's soul, his progress through Paradise entails the gradual perfecting of his spiritual vision. So far, in the planetary heavens, Dante has been shown the spiritual nature of human life. Now he is about to see the spiritual life as it exists in eternity, no longer a subjectively felt experience, but an objective truth in visible form. In the planetary heavens Dante met spirits, talked with them, and learned a great deal about spiritual truths as they apply to human existence. Even the symbols he encountered - the double crown, the cross, the eagle, and the ladder - expressed some truth about wisdom, courage, justice, and contemplation. In the last three heavens, however, he will not so much learn about spiritual truth as come in direct contact with it. He will have to deal with it as an objective thing. But before he can do so, before he can fully enter into the heavenly life, he must take stock of himself and know who he is. That is why, in the fixed stars, he is placed in the constellation which rained its influence on the earth at the time of his birth and made him the particular individual he is. And that is why, too, Beatrice makes him look back, to see how far he has traveled. What Dante sees as he looks down from Gemini is not so much the architecture of the universe as the path of his spiritual progress. Silently looking upon that path, he takes full possession of himself, and is then ready for the test that awaits him.

CANTO 23

Beatrice looks eastward, and soon Dante sees the heavens shine more and more brilliantly as Christ and the host of the redeemed approach. The light shining from Christ is so intensely bright that, like lightning bursting from a cloud, Dante's mind bursts its bonds and loses itself. Beatrice calls him back to himself and tells him that now, strengthened by the vision of Christ, he is able to sustain her smile. He is not, however, able to sustain the sight of the Redeemer for long, and when he once again looks at the procession, Christ, in his mercy, has withdrawn above and merely shines upon his redeemed. Among them, Beatrice points out the Virgin Mary and the Apostles (the Rose and the Lillies). As Dante drinks in the sight of the Blessed Virgin, whom he refers to as the "living star" which conquers in Heaven as it conquers on earth, he hears a beautiful melody. That music comes from a circle of light which has descended from above and is circling around the Virgin. The light announces itself as the archangel Gabriel, who sings her praises and invites her to rejoin her Son in the highest heaven. At this point the Virgin rises out of sight through the Primum Mobile as the souls of the redeemed sing the hymn Regina coeli ("O Queen of Heaven").

Comment

As suggested in the preceding commentary, Dante's journey through Paradise has so far been a preparation for Redemption - it was designed to perfect his soul. In the heaven where the triumph of Christ is manifested in the procession of the redeemed, Dante is going to be questioned on the heavenly virtues which lead to salvation. But salvation is a gift of divine grace - a gift personified, so to speak, in Christ. That is why Christ shines down on the host of the redeemed after he has removed to the Empyrean; that is why, too, Dante's vision of him strengthens him sufficiently to sustain once again Beatrice's smile - i.e., to come close to his goal in the Empyrean.

CANTO 24

Beatrice now asks the spirits of the redeemed to let Dante partake of the blessings of divine knowledge which they enjoy in Paradise. The saints, in their ecstasy, form circles of whirling lights, and St. Peter sweeps out from the brightest circle in answer to Beatrice's request. She asks him to test Dante on faith. Questioned by Peter, Dante follows the Epistle to the Hebrews (attributed to St. Paul) in defining faith; it is, he says, "the substance of things hoped for, and the evidence of things unseen." Peter then asks him why it is placed first among substances and then categorized as evidence. Dante explains that the "deep things" of heaven revealed to him in Paradise are so hidden from mortal sight that they exist on earth only in man's belief in them. Hope being built on that belief, faith is the foundation of hope, and therefore a substance (in the sense of "standing under" as a support.) But, Dante continues, this belief is the starting-point for a line of reasoning about the nature of things unseen; hence faith is also to be defined as the "argument" or evidence for the unknown.

Peter is pleased with Dante's definition, and then questions Dante about his own faith. Here Dante declares that his faith is unquestioning, based on Scripture, and that the truth of Scripture is authenticated for him by God's miracles, the greatest of which, he says, is the fact that Christianity spread without the need of any miracle. Finally, when asked about the content of his faith, Dante asserts his faith in God, whom he defines first as the unmoved mover who moves the heavens with longing and desire, and then as three Persons in one Essence. Proof for the first, he says, is to be found in Aristotle's Physics and Metaphysics as well as in Scripture; the second is to be found only in Scripture. Peter, delighted with Dante's confession of faith, circles him three times.

CANTO 25

Dante's declaration of faith has earned him Peter's blessing, and Dante now declares that if his poem ever melts the cruelty of the Florentines who sent him into exile, he will take the poet's laurel crown at the font where he was baptized. After this preliminary remark, a second light joins Dante, St. Peter, and Beatrice. It is St. James, who proceeds to question Dante on hope. First Beatrice declares that the Church Militant has no child richer in hope than Dante. It is for that very hope that he has been granted the privilege of his vision of Heaven before his death. As for the nature and source of hope, she adds, Dante will speak for himself. Hope, Dante declares at this point, is a "sure expectation of future glory, the product of divine grace and precedent merit." Its source is in Scripture, he adds, and he refers specifically to the ninth Psalm and the Epistle of James (i:12). James now asks to hear the content of Dante's hope, and Dante answers that in Isaiah (lxi:7, 10) and Revelation (vii:9) he reads the promise of the resurrection of the body as well as the immortality of the soul.

A third light now joins Peter and James. It is as bright as the sun, and Beatrice tells Dante it is St. John. As Dante strains his eyes to see the saint's body, he is blinded by the brilliance of the light. John reminds him that his body is dust and awaits the general resurrection: Only Christ and Mary, the saint declares, rose to heaven with their bodies. Suddenly the music is stilled, and the blinded Dante looks to Beatrice for comfort, but in vain.

PARADISO

. . . .

CANTO 26

John reassures Dante by telling him that Beatrice has the power to restore his lost sight, and suggests that in the meantime they discourse of love. Questioned about the object of his love, Dante declares it to be God, who is the beginning and the end of all his loves. The primary reason for loving God, Dante continues, is that God is good, and the good, once known, must of necessity be desired. Aristotle and Scripture have made him understand this truth. But John wishes to know what other reasons, besides the fact that God is good in Himself, Dante has for loving God. Here Dante mentions the creation of the world, his own creation, Christ's sacrifice on the Cross, and man's hope of heaven. These instances of God's good to mankind are all secondary reasons for loving him. When Dante has finished, a hymn of praise to God is heard, and his sight is restored to him.

As Dante recovers the use of his eyes he notices a fourth light that has joined the group he is standing in. The new arrival,

Beatrice tells him, is Adam, and Dante eagerly directs his silent questioning to the first father of the human race. Adam first tells Dante that his banishment from the earthly paradise was due not so much to his having eaten the forbidden fruit as to his having disobeyed God's command. He then tells the poet that he lived for 930 years, and spent 4032 years in Limbo. As for the language he spoke, it had died out long before the tower of Babel was built. Lastly, his stay in the Garden of Eden lasted little more than six hours.

Comment

Until his arrival in the eighth heaven, Dante has been the one to ask questions and garner knowledge from the answers. Here, on the threshold of final Revelation, it is he who is questioned by Peter, James, and John, the historical representatives, as it were, of the three heavenly virtues. His qualifications as a true Christian deserving to become part of the body of the Church Triumphant in the Emyprean are being tested as he is asked to express his understanding of the three virtues and specify the content of his own faith, hope, and charity.

Faith, as the Middle Ages saw it, is not blind. On the contrary, it is an intellectual process by which the nature of the unknown is reasonably ascertained, and it underlies the other two virtues which are built on it - hence Dante terms it a substance. In content it is the intellectual belief in the existence of an unmoved mover of all things, one Being who yet manifests himself as three Persons: Father, Son, and Holy Ghost. It is the foundation of the Christian life, and Dante's unhesitating confession of his faith to Peter earns him the saint's blessing, expressed by Peter's circling round him three times.

Hope, like faith, is not blind; it is based on the very faith Dante has acknowledged and is directed specifically to the expectation of eternal life, both in body and in soul. And lastly, love is the desire for the supreme good which is God, a desire which is automatically born out of the belief in and hope for it. As a secondary aspect it also directs itself to the Creation, made lovable because it reflects in some measure the beauty of the Creator. And it also contains gratitude to the Creator for the act of creation without which the intelligence and sensibility of a Dante capable of loving the Creator and his Creation would never have come into being.

Dante's temporary blindness in connection with his desire to see St. John's body bears on a medieval legend, only partly accepted by the Western Church, according to which the saint's body was translated to heaven at the time of his death. St. Thomas Aquinas accepted it merely as a "pious belief," and Dante here sets out to deny it categorically. But his blindness also indicates a temporary loss of spiritual bearings. Having declared his hope in the resurrection of the body, he is so engrossed in desire for the body that he loses sight of the supreme source of love, which is God. His discourse with John restores the proper perspective, and that perspective restores his sight to him.

The fact that Adam joins the three saints in discourse with Dante may seem puzzling at first, but the first father's appearance in the heaven of the fixed stars is not an irrelevancy. This is the heaven where the triumph of Christ the Redeemer is manifested, and it is only appropriate that the first soul to be saved - Adam, who was rescued by Christ from Limbo - should make an appearance in this heaven. Furthermore, as the archetypical representative of humanity, he sums up in his being and experience the perfection and experience of mankind, Dante's included. In Adam's discourse, Dante's thesis of the cause of sin is confirmed: Not the eating of the forbidden fruit, but disobedience caused the Fall. In other words, man sinned when his will no longer harmonized with the will of his Maker. And Dante has no illusions about human nature, since he allows man a bare six hours of innocence in the Garden of Eden before his will begins to exert itself in directions contrary to the will of God.

CANTO 27

After Adam's speech, Dante says, all Paradise burst into song praising the Father, the Son, and the Holy Ghost. Then St. Peter turns red with anger as he denounces Pope Boniface VIII, whom he terms a usurper. At his words all heaven changes color and Beatrice blushes for shame. Peter then continues his denunciation, contrasting the spirituality of ancient popes with the greed and ambition of modern popes, such as Clement V and John XXII. But, Peter declares, the wrongs shall soon be righted by Providence, and he bids Dante report what he has heard in Heaven when he returns to earth.

The spirits, like so many flakes of snow, now float upwards to the highest heaven, and Beatrice once again has Dante look down towards the earth. Looking down, Dante becomes aware of the speed with which the eighth heaven has been moving: Only part of the earth visible to him is now illuminated by the sun; the rest of this "threshing-floor" is in darkness. When Dante looks back to Beatrice, the power of her smile raises him to the ninth heaven, the Primum Mobile. There, in the swiftest of the heavens, Beatrice explains that the Primum Mobile is the starting point of the universe. Space and time have their roots in it and take their measure from it. Beyond it, they do not exist, for it is surrounded only by divine light and love. And Beatrice then turns her thoughts to the earth, where faith and innocence are found only in little children, and where covetousness turns mankind from white to black from the day of its birth. This degeneracy is due solely to the fact that there is none to govern the earth, she adds; but this lack will soon be remedied and mankind will be set on a straight course.

CANTO 28

Seeing a reflection in Beatrice's eyes, Dante turns around to look at a point of extremely intense light with nine concentric circles revolving around it; the closer the circles are to the center, the more brightly they shine and the more swiftly they revolve. Beatrice tells Dante that the universe - heaven and nature - hangs on that point, and that it is love which makes the circles revolve. Dante understands that the circles represent the angelic intelligences who govern the heavenly spheres, but he objects that the universe presents the reverse pattern: the more divine heavens are further removed from the center. He therefore asks why the copy - i.e., the physical universe - does not follow the pattern of the model. Beatrice explains that, since the substance of the heavens is uniform, the larger the heaven, the greater its excellence. Similarly, swiftness and brightness measure the excellence of the angelic circles, and the outermost circle of the universe thus corresponds in excellence to the angelic circle that loves and knows the most. As Beatrice finishes her explanation the circles shoot off sparks, and Hosannas are heard moving from circle to circle to that central point which holds all in place for all eternity. Beatrice then enumerates the nine orders of angels, beginning with those who, closest to God, sink their sight most deeply into the "truth wherein every intellect is stilled," and she takes this occasion to inform Dante of the fact that blessedness is founded on the intellectual act of knowledge, and not on love, which follows from knowledge. The angelic orders, corresponding (in reverse order) to the nine heavens, are the Seraphim, Cherubim, and Thrones; Dominations, Virtues, and Powers; Principalities, Archangels, and Angels. Such was the order revealed to Dionysius by his own enraptured vision and the instruction he received from St. Paul, who had himself seen Heaven before his death.

CANTO 29

For a moment Beatrice gazes on the point of light in which is centered, as she puts it, every "where" and every "when." She knows what Dante's questions are, and she proceeds to satisfy his curiosity about the angels, whose realm the ninth heaven is. To begin with, she tells Dante that God brought life into being so that His reflected light might enjoy conscious existence, not in order to acquire further good for Himself. Furthermore, it is pointless to wonder what God may have done before, since the concepts of before and after do not exist outside the created universe. Creation itself was instantaneous and simultaneous: Pure form or act (the angels), pure matter or potency (prime matter), and the conjoined form and matter (the physical heavens) came into being at one and the same time. Jerome erred, she added, when he said that the angels were created a long time before the creation of the universe. Beatrice then further informs Dante of the fall of the angels. They fell right after their creation, before one could count twenty, and they fell because of Lucifer's - i.e., Satan's - pride. Those who did not fall were less presumptuous and modest enough to acknowledge God as the source of their being and their vast understanding. They received illuminating grace and, accepting it, increased their merit; grace and merit both exalted their vision and they were confirmed. No more would need to be said about the angels, Beatrice concludes, if not for the erroneous teaching of the schools, which assign them the faculty of memory in addition to understanding and will. Since they have their vision ever fixed on God, from whom nothing is concealed, angels, she declares, have no need of memory.

Her correction of the schools' teaching leads Beatrice into a digression in which she deplores the errors of human speculation (often due to ignorance) and condemns the distortion of Scripture by vainglorious preachers more anxious to impress their audience than to spread knowledge of the truth. Returning to the angels, Beatrice explains that their number exceeds any to be conceived by the human mind, but that each angel has his own specific insight and quality of love resulting from it. And she ends by declaring that the extent of God's quality may be seen in the fact that His light has made itself so many mirrors to reflect it individually without losing its essential unity.

Comment

Dante's intense interest in angels may be peculiarly medieval; nonetheless, it becomes meaningful once we call to mind that the angelic intelligences are the assurance, as it were, of the spiritual nature of the universe. The question of the order of creation is then no longer picayune and Dante must insist that the universe sprang into being in one creative act; it was created material and spiritual at once, and one aspect is not to be separated from the other.

Pure form is termed "act" because everything contained in the angelic intelligence is existent as an actuality at all times, always fully realized. Matter on the other hand, has "potency" in the sense that it holds the potentiality of being molded by form. The terms belong to the technical vocabulary of scholastic philosophy.

One last point about Dante's unerring tact as a poet. He quite appropriately refuses to reduce the angelic intelligences to the level of human beings and so, instead of the ludicrous spectacle of interviews between himself and the angels, he has Beatrice interpret the phenomena he perceives in the ninth heaven.

PARADISO

CANTOS 30-33

. . . .

CANTO 30

Just as when the sun rises in the sky, the stars disappear from sight, so the nine concentric circles fade from Dante's view. Constrained by love to turn his eyes to Beatrice, he now finds her resplendent with such incomparable beauty that his powers as a poet fail him. She, for her part, tells Dante that they have now reached the Empyrean, the heaven that is pure light - "an intellectual light that is full of love, a love of the true good that is charged with gladness, gladness that transcends every sweetness." Here he shall see the angels and the redeemed as they will appear after the Last Judgment. A sudden flash of blinding light enfolds Dante who, upon hearing that each soul is so received in the Empyrean, feels his strength exceed his own power so that nothing can now overpower his sight. The first thing Dante sees is a river of light running between two banks covered with grass and flowers. From the river issue sparks which drop into the blossoms on the banks and then plunge back into the stream. Beatrice now speaks again and tells Dante that what he sees is the last symbolic disguise of the final reality, which he will see only after he "drinks" (with his eyes) of the "water" of that stream. As he gazes intently into the stream, Dante sees it change shape into a vast heavenly rose composed of the ranks of the redeemed. They are illuminated by the light of God which, reflected by the Primum Mobile, gives them the strength to look directly at God Himself.

As Dante stares at the rows and rows of redeemed souls, Beatrice points out one vacant place which, she says, is reserved for the emperor Henry VII, who shall come to set Italy straight before she is ready. But the Italians will reject him, and Pope Clement V will plot against him, yet shortly after Henry's death, the Pope will be thrust down to Hell, in the circle of the simonists.

Comment

The river of light is the last symbolic representation Dante encounters on his journey. A symbol of divine grace, it still sets redemption in the context of time (the flow of the river suggests the flow of time); the sparks are the angels and the flowers the redeemed. Dante must drink in this image before his mind is ready for the higher conception of eternity; as his eyes become satiated, the Church Triumphant is revealed to his sight: The river transforms itself into the white rose of heavenly love which houses the souls of the redeemed.

Beatrice's last words to Dante indicate, for the last time in *the Divine Comedy*, the direct connection between the heavenly Jerusalem and the ideal order for the world below. Her brief eulogy of the emperor Henry, on whom Dante had pinned his hopes, coming hard on her reference to "our city" - meaning the heavenly rose - indicates the relationship between an ideal

Empire on earth and the triumph of mankind in Heaven. The point is all the more forcefully made by the disdainful dismissal of Clement V to Hell, which follows the praise of Henry. (For Clement's place among the simonists, see *Inferno*, Canto 19.)

CANTO 31

The Church Triumphant, consisting of all the souls redeemed by Christ, is seen as a huge white rose, with the redeemed themselves forming the petals. The angels fly from God to the rose and back, proffering peace and ardor to the souls, without intercepting the light emanating from God or interfering with the souls' sight of the Creator. Turning to Beatrice, Dante finds her gone; an old man is standing in her place. To Dante's question, "Where is she?" the old man answers that he has come at Beatrice's request to guide Dante's desire to its goal; Beatrice herself has resumed her place in the rose and Dante may see her there. Gazing at her in her place of glory, Dante expresses his gratitude and his hope that the love she has engendered in him may keep him worthy of her to the end of his life. As Beatrice hears his prayer, she smiles at him from her place in the rose, and then turns to God. The elderly man, who identifies himself as St. Bernard, now urges Dante to prepare himself for the consummation of his wishes by first carefully examining the divine rose; the Queen of Heaven, he declares, will grant them every grace because Bernard is her faithful devotee. Upon learning who his companion is, Dante gazes in awe at the man who, through the force of contemplation, had seen God while yet on earth. Bernard, however, calls the poet's attention to the rose, and especially to the glorified Virgin Mother at the center, blazing in light amidst numberless rejoicing angels. Her smile, Dante says, brings gladness to the eyes of the other saints in the rose, and Dante himself, seeing the love with which Bernard turns to her, is inspired with even greater ardor in his adoration.

Comment

St. Bernard is the third of Dante's guides on his spiritual pilgrimage to God. This mystic contemplation which alone can bring one to God (hence the medieval speculation about his having seen God while still alive), his life-long devotion to the cult of Mary, which he fostered, makes him the perfect intercessor for Dante's wish to still his desire by looking on the deity. He does not explain or teach, as Virgil and Beatrice have done. He merely directs Dante's own prayer to the Virgin Mary by adding his own to it.

Mary herself is important here, since it is she who takes on herself the task of mediating between mankind and the Redeemer. The image of ideal motherhood undoubtedly assigned that task to her - the mother's sympathy and love for her faltering child serves to cancel out the legacy of sin left by that other great mother, Eve. (The Eve - Mary contrast was a commonplace of medieval thought, and is reflected in the following canto in Eve's position beneath Mary in the rose.) Lastly, we must not forget that it was at the Virgin's instigation that Dante's pilgrimage was made possible: She dispatched St. Lucy to Beatrice, who then sought out Virgil in Limbo. Corresponding to the Holy Trinity of Father, Son, and Holy Ghost, there is, in *the Divine Comedy*, a Marian trinity consisting of the Blessed Virgin, St. Lucy, and Beatrice - the feminine object of love which directs Dante's passion to God.

CANTO 32

Bernard now indicates to Dante divisions of the great rose he has been gazing at. The rose is divided downwards into two halves; the one half holding those who believed in Christ to come, the other reserved for those who believed in Christ come. In the first half, at the dividing line, is found Mary, with Eve at her feet; beneath them are Rachel, with Beatrice on the same level with her, Sarah, Rebecca, Judith, and Ruth. On the other side of Mary is John the Baptist, and under him Sts. Francis, Benedict, and Augustine. Further down are found the children who were saved, not through merit of their own, because they died before they could exercise free choice, but on account of the faith and observances of their parents. And lest Dante should be perplexed, St. Bernard explains that God grants grace in accordance with his judgment, even before birth: He illustrates the point by referring to the Biblical story of Jacob and Esau, according to which Esau had God's enmity while in his mother's womb.

Dante's gaze returns to Mary, in front of whom Gabriel is seen exulting. After looking at several others in the rose - Adam, St. Peter, St. John, Moses, Anna (mother of Mary), and St. Lucy, Dante is bid to turn in prayer to the Virgin Mary so that he may receive from her the final grace of being able to look directly at the source of all Creation.

CANTO 33

"Virgin Mother, daughter of thy son" - so St. Bernard opens his prayer asking Mary to grant Dante the strength to look upon God. His prayer is first in praise of Mary, the tender, pitying mother who brings hope and mercy to all mankind. Let her scatter, the saint asks, the clouds of Dante's mortality, so that he may partake of the supreme joy of gazing at the divine essence. Let her also, after so great a vision, keep his affections sound. Bernard asks this for Dante, and so do Beatrice and many other saints, who have folded their hands in prayer with him. Mary turns to God, and Bernard indicates to Dante that the request has been granted; but Dante, carried by his strong desire, has already moved his eyes to the "ray of deep light which in itself is true." From the moment on, Dante says, his vision, his power to see, was stronger than anything human speech can express, and all that his mind retains is the impression of a dream.

Dante first sees a light which so holds his attention that he cannot possibly look away - looking at it joins him to the infinite Virtue. Within the light Dante sees all parts of the universe bound together by love. Looking more deeply, he then sees three rings of the same size but of three different colors - the first is reflected by the second, and the third is a fire issuing equally from the other two. The second ring seems to contain a human effigy, and Dante strains to see how the human image is conjoined with the divine ring, but he is not up to such a task. A sudden flash opens his mind to the mystery, and he perceives the truth. Here, Dante concludes, the power to express the great vision perceived by his mind failed him; but already his will and desire, like a wheel spinning evenly, were turned by the Love that moves the sun and the other stars.

Comment

Dante has reached his goal, and the mystic vision, so clearly expressed by the **imagery** of light of the last canto, brings him the final peace wherein his will and desire become one with the will and desire of God - moved by the Love which unites and regulates the entire universe. The vision itself is over, but the peace remains, together with the reminder to be found in the "stars" with which *Paradiso*, like *Inferno* and *Purgatorio* in this respect, closes. In the first two parts of *the Divine Comedy* the stars were an indication of the goal to be reached; here they stand as a living reminder of the consummation achieved in Paradise.

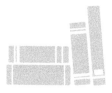

THE DIVINE COMEDY BY DANTE

THE CONVIVIO

The Convivio, probably completed around 1308, is an extension into philosophy of the experience dealt with in *the Vita Nuova*. It is a treatise in which Dante's contemporaries are invited to share his learning: his wisdom was imparted in his odes, but now, Dante declares, he finds that they need to be interpreted both literally and allegorically if they are to be understood. It is this interpretation which he undertakes in *the Convivio*, which originally was to consist of fifteen books, an introduction, and commentaries on fourteen canzoni, or odes. These odes appear to be impassioned love poems, but, Dante asserts, their meaning is allegorical and must, therefore, be interpreted lest his passion be misinterpreted. Such is the design of this book, which sought to impart knowledge not in the medieval language of learning, Latin, but in the vernacular Italian, so that it might truly reach a wide audience. Actually, the work was never completed, for Dante wrote only four books - the introduction and three commentaries.

THE DIVINE COMEDY BY DANTE

THE LATIN WORKS

....

Of the Latin works, only the *De Vulgari Eloquentia* and *the De Monarchia* need be mentioned here. The former is a treatise, probably written around 1304 and also unfinished, defending the use of the vernacular - in this case, Italian - as a vehicle for serious poetry. In it Dante seeks to teach the correct use of Italian in poetry, and sets forth rules for the classification and selection of words to achieve a varied and pleasing **diction**. This little treatise is also a manual on the art of poetry since it takes up such questions as the proper **themes** for the various types of poetry, the different forms of poetry, the relation between style and form, as well as problems of versification.

The De Monarchia, Dante's treatise on politics, has been discussed in connection with the political scheme of *the Divine Comedy*, and nothing need be added here. Its dating is problematical, but evidence points to late composition, at least after *the Convivio*.

THE DIVINE COMEDY BY DANTE

CRITICAL COMMENTARY

· ·

When one considers that Dante criticism began in the fourteenth century, and has grown unabated ever since, the task of surveying so vast a body of scholarship and criticism may well seem staggering. Dominant tendencies in interpretation, however, may be readily discerned in different ages, and it is these that are delineated in the following brief sketch. Those seeking fuller, more detailed information are advised to consult the bibliographical listings in Barbi's *Life of Dante* (trans. Paul Ruggiers), Bergin's *Dante*, Cosmo's *A Handbook to Dante Studies*, and Vittorini's *The Age of Dante*. For more specialized works the student is referred to the bibliography drawn up by J. E. Spingarn for the English-language edition of *Vossler's Mediaeval Culture* and, specially, the catalogue of *Cornell University's Fiske Collection* published by T. W. Koch (Catalogue of the Dante Collection presented by W. Fiske to Cornell University - 2 vols.) as well as the Additions ... 1898–1920 by M. Fowler. Two very useful historical surveys of the evolution of Dante's reputation in the major Western European countries and the United States are to be found in Werner P. Friederich's *Dante's Fame Abroad*, 1350–1850, and Angelina LaPiana's

Dante's American Pilgrimages. Any or all of the above will guide the student in search of fuller information than can be provided here.

The history of Dante criticism is, in a sense, the story of Dante's reputation through the ages. *The Divine Comedy* spread Dante's fame in Italy in his lifetime; and shortly after his death there began to appear the fourteenth-century biographies and commentaries that formed the beginning of the steady stream of exegetical and critical publications devoted to the Florentinei poet. The result has been cumulative body of interpretation that has developed over the centuries.

To Dante's contemporaries the allegorical nature of *the Divine Comedy* was self-evident - the allegorical cast of mind was one of the characteristics of medieval culture. It is therefore immaterial whether or not the early commentators - men such as Jacopo and Pietro Alighieri (Dante's two sons), Jacopo della Lana, Boccaccio, Filippo Villani, and the so-called Anonimo Fiorentino - were acquainted with the letter to Can Grande della Scala, Lord of Verona, in which, dedicating the *Paradiso* to this prince, Dante explicitly asserted the four-tiered allegorical nature of his poem. We, today, may find that this assertion justifies the allegorical interpretation: Dante's contemporaries and near-contemporaries merely took such interpretation for granted. They naturally also took for granted the **didactic** nature of the poem, and thus bent their efforts to the elucidation of the text. Not only did they seek to set forth the moral, philosophical, and theological allegorism of the poem but, since Dante had made himself its hero, they more than once tended to link the moral of an **episode** to biographical fact.

In insisting, by their example, on the hidden meanings behind the literal statement, and in drawing on the life of the author - hero for the clarification of the moral significance of episodes, these early commentators may have done no more than follow Dante's lead in the light of the received ideas of their time. But they also, in effect, laid out the main directions of Dante scholarship for subsequent ages. The numerous annotated editions of *the Divine Comedy* brought out over the centuries both in Italy and elsewhere have concerned themselves with explicating details for the comprehension of the general reader, and the bulk of Dantean criticism consists of so many attempts to define the "true" meaning or meanings to be found in the poem. The early commentators sought to do just that, moved by the very enthusiasm that has inspired all subsequent admirers of Dante to comment on his works.

The initial enthusiasm for Dante's great poem died down by the middle of the sixteenth century. Commentators and printers did manage to preserve its fame in Italy up to that time, but the decline had already begun to set in a century before. Attacks against it were launched in the fifteenth century by some of the classical humanists, whose total dedication to the recovery of classical culture led them to disparage Dante's masterpiece.

Typical of their attitude is the contemptuous statement of the early Florentine humanist Niccolo Niccoli (1364–1467) to the effect that *the Divine Comedy* was a poem for bakers and cobblers because it was written in the vulgar tongue (i.e., Italian) and not Latin. True, there were other humanists who still admired the poem, the most notable among them being Cristoforo Landino, whose famous Commentary appeared with the first Florentine edition in 1481. Nonetheless, Dante was more and more felt to be a man of the past, whose work did not conform to the rising canons of the taste of neo-classicism. By the time we reach the seventeenth century his fame had reached its lowest point - the fact that, in Italy, only three editions of *the*

Divine Comedy were published during that century, as against thirty in the sixteenth, thirty-one in the eighteenth, and about 320 in the nineteenth centuries is sufficient evidence. Typical of the disfavor in which Dante found himself is Fulvio Frugoni's declaration (*Ritratti critici*, 1669) that he could appreciate one **stanza** from the great lyricists of his century more than the whole of *the Divine Comedy*.

It has been pointed out that the low ebb of Dante's literary reputation was in some measure due to the influence of the Jesuits and the Counter-Reformation. *The De Monarchia* (written to challenge papal claims to temporal supremacy) was placed on the Church's Index Librorum Prohibitorum (*Index of Forbidden Books*) in 1564; in a supplement to the Index published in Lisbon in 1581 parts of *the Divine Comedy* itself and of Landino's commentary were added as well. Protestants, on the other hand, on the rare occasions when they made use of Dante's works in their polemics against the Papacy, showed no more interest in the literary value of *the Divine Comedy* than their Jesuit enemies. In short, a combination of changing tastes and near-political motives contributed to the demise of genuine interest in Dante's masterpiece.

If Dante's fame was kept alive in Italy into the middle of the sixteenth century - and the Italians could scarcely ignore the man who fashioned a literary language for them - no such development took place outside his native land. With the exception of Chaucer in England and, two centuries later, Marguerite de Navarre in France, the English and French showed little interest in Dante. In the seventeenth century, as has already been noted, it was the enemy of papal pretensions that Reformers, Huguenots, and Protestants were interested in, not the creator of a literary masterpiece. And with the rise of neo-classicism Dante stood little chance of recovering from the literary disrepute that he had fallen into. It is only in the eighteenth century that his stock began to rise, and, paradoxical as it may seem, it is then that the most violent neo-classical attacks were mounted against him. The paradox is readily understandable, however; as literary sensibility slowly began to shift in the direction of what became Romanticism, the neo-classicists manned their forts to defend the established positions. And although Dante was scarcely mentioned in the famous *Battle of the Ancients and the Moderns*, it is nonetheless the partisans of the moderns who paved the way for the revival of his reputation in the nineteenth century.

The European neo-classical position is best exemplified by Voltaire (1694–1778). Essentially, he did not understand Dante's poem, which he repeatedly characterized as "bizarre." It seemed to him to fit no known literary category, and although he had some faint words of praise for Dante's language and for the occasional "natural beauties" of the poem (*Essai sur les moeurs*, 1756), and although the anti-clericalist in him responded to the poet who put popes in Hell, his final judgment nonetheless remained that the subject of the poem was in bad taste and that Dante's reputation among his admirers was based on the fact that no one read the poem through. (It should be noted here that the evidence indicates that Voltaire himself must have read the poem very superficially.) "The Italians call him divine," he wrote in his *Dictionnaire philosophique* (1764), "but his is a hidden divinity: few understand his oracles; he has commentators, and that is perhaps one more reason for his not being understood. His reputation will always be championed because no one reads him." And after a flippant summary of *Inferno*, Voltaire concluded ironically that "this hodgepodge has been deemed a beautiful epic poem."

Voltaire's renewed attack in the *Lettres chinoises* of 1776 perhaps indicates most clearly what it was that shocked him in *the Divine Comedy*. Again he bestowed some lukewarm praise for occasionally striking passages while disparaging the poem in a mocking tone for its oddities, its admixture of paganism and Christianity, its episodic quality - all of which, he declared, end up by making the reader tired. His classically nurtured mind, his classically trained sensibility, and his rationalism were all offended by the "Gothic" extravagance of the medieval poem, its emphasis on the truth of the supernatural and the consequent de-emphasis of purely limited earthly values, its mysticism, and its occasional "crudity." These were intrinsically foreign to Voltaire's nature and thus ruled out anything but a final negative response to Dante's work.

In his response to *the Divine Comedy* Voltaire typified the attitude of eighteenth-century neo-classicists, and his great prestige throughout Europe lent weight to the attacks launched against Dante's poem. As has already been noted, these attacks were in fact defensive, opposed to the slow but nonetheless perceptible rise of Dante's reputation, especially in Italy. One such attack is noteworthy because it created a veritable scandal in Italy and forced Dante's defenders to re-examine their position and set their claims for his greatness on solid ground. In 1758 the Italian Jesuit dilettante Saverio Bettinelli published, as an appendix to a collection of poetry, the so-called *Lettere virgiliane* (Virgilian letters) in which Virgil himself lashed out at Dante and condemned *the Divine Comedy*. Like Voltaire before and after him, Bettinelli based his judgment on the tastes and prejudices of the Age of Enlightenment; implicit in his strictures is the notion that poetry should above all else delight the reader's imagination with the beauty of the things depicted, move his heart with the sweetness of the sentiments expressed, and please his ear with the musical harmony of the verses. This notion had as its corollary the requirement for the kind of surface clarity that makes the work immediately understandable; it did not seem possible that enjoyment could be found in patiently working one's way through a poem. Therefore, while Bettinelli, too, admitted the presence of a few beautiful passages (he specifically mentioned the Francesca da Rimini and Count Ugolino **episodes** of *Inferno*), he condemned the bulk of *Inferno* for its obscurity and extravagance. As for Purgatorio and Paradiso, they fared even worse, for they were not even allowed the redeeming moments of beauty of the first canticle. Bettinelli was apparently willing to grant Dante talent, however: perhaps, he declared through his mouthpiece Virgil, if Dante had lived in better times he would have been the greatest of poets, for "Dante lacked nothing but good taste and discernment in matters of art."

The statement of Bettinelli just quoted marks the low point, in a way, of Dante's literary reputation. Actually his fame was already on the rise. Earlier in the century, the great Italian philosopher Giovanni Battista Vico (1668–1744), whose work was to influence the German Romantics, had begun the task of rehabilitating Dante. Both in the *Scienza Nuova* (New Science) and *the Giudizio sopra Dante* (Judgment on Dante), Vico presented Dante as the Italian Homer, towering against the back-drop of medieval Italy. In other words, he restored Dante to a position where he could be appreciated for his true merits; he explained the poet and his work historically, setting both against the cultural and historical background of their time. But he also saw him as a gigantic genius, primitive, emotional, but powerful in his creative force, whose work, poor in ethical and logical thought, does not appeal to reason but is alive with vital energy. Vico therefore also felt that Dante's learning was a distinct disadvantage to him, and if one is to speak justly of him one must stress only his poetic expressiveness. True, Vico's judgment in large measure fell on deaf ears; in this, as in the other aspects of his thought, he was not recognized at his true value until the Romantic Age. Nonetheless, he traced the path and set the direction for the bulk of the critical discussion that was to come in the nineteenth century; he single-handedly, in effect, defined the problems to be taken up by subsequent Dante criticism.

The scholars and critics who rose to the defense of Dante after Bettinelli's nasty pamphlet followed, albeit unwittingly, the leads provided earlier in the century by Vico. The first to reply, Gasparo Gozzi, in what has come to be known as the *Difesa di Dante* (Defense of Dante, 1758), took Bettinelli to task both for the superficiality of his reading of Dante and for his motives in writing a piece of purely destructive criticism. Others, contradicting Bettinelli, insisted on the many beauties to be found in Dante; others still, on the poet's creative genius. But if a dominant trend comes into view, it is that associated with the Risorgimento, the movement of national political and cultural revival that eventually led to the unification of Italy. Consequently Dante appeared as the great Italian patriot, the uncompromising foe of the Papacy's interference in the political life of Italy; his poem was likewise read primarily as a political allegory with anticlerical overtones. In this connection mention should be made of Gabriele Rossetti's interpretation (in publications between 1826 and 1842) of the *Divine Comedy* as allegory in a very special sense: according to him the mysterious passages in the poem were so many secret messages addressed to a subversive international association, heretical in character, that was dedicated to the religious and political overthrow of the Church of Rome. While this view was categorically rejected by most European critics, it has occasionally appeared in one guise or another, e.g., attempts to link Dante with the Catharist heresy.

Aside from involvement with the Risorgimento - primarily an Italian affair - pre-Romantic and Romantic interest in Dante centered on two things: curiosity about medieval lore and Christian poetry, and enthusiasm for the individualistic man of genius. The latter accounts for the nineteenth-century view of Dante as pathfinder and hero of poetry. Characteristic of this view are Macaulay's various essays in which he touched on Dante ("Criticisms on the Principal Italian Writers," *Knight's Quarterly Magazine*, 1824; "Essay on Milton," *Edinburgh Review*, 1825; "Essay on Machiavelli," 1827; etc.), and Carlyle's lecture on Dante in his Lectures in the History of Literature (1838) as well as his discussion of Dante in the third chapter, "The Hero as Poet," of his famous *On Heroes, Hero-Worship, and the Heroic in History* (1841). But the outstanding Dantist among nineteenth-century critics was the Italian critic De Sanctis. His view of Dante was fundamentally that of Vico (though he substituted Shakespeare for Homer in the comparison); he insisted on a close reading of Dante's text, without benefit of preconceived notions or commentaries - the poet, on the strength of his art, would come through to the reader willing to undertake the task with an open and even doubting mind. De Sanctis in effect rejected allegorical and/or ideological readings of *the Divine Comedy*, and while he did not deny Dante's intellectual intentions in the poem, he firmly believed that those intentions had little to do with the results actually achieved - results due to the superb poetic genius of the artist, not the intellectual doctrine of the abstract thinker.

Arch-Romantic in its glorification of the creative genius of Dante, in its emphasis on the poem as a work of art rather than a compendium of medieval doctrine, De Sanctis' view may be termed anti-scholarly. The scholars of the nineteenth century, on the other hand, did not become involved in the controversy over esthetic criticism of *the Divine Comedy* - the battle between neo-Classicists and Romantics simply did not concern them. Their efforts were bent to the establishing of a text, setting it in its historical context (political and cultural), clarifying the obscurities, explaining allusions, references, etc. Here such names as Witte, in Germany, Moore, in England, and Scartazzini in Switzerland come to mind. But the culmination of this scholarly-historical movement in Dante criticism may be found in Karl Vossler's *Mediaeval Culture: An Introduction to Dante and His Times* (1929), first published (1907–1910) in Germany under the title of *Die Gottliche Komodie* (*The Divine Comedy*). In this exhaustive study Vossler undertook to set the poem fully against the background of medieval culture - religion, philosophy, ethics, politics, and literature - before coming to an examination of the poem itself qua poem. What Vossler sought to do was to reconcile the two main schools of criticism - the esthetic and the scholarly - historical, yet his effort at uniting these ultimately fails as the part devoted to *the Divine Comedy* proper does not naturally grow out of the preceding detailed examination of the various facets of medieval culture. In the final analysis Vossler still presents Dante's poem in terms of a struggle between intellectualism and poetry.

Twentieth-century interpretations of *the Divine Comedy* tend, on the whole, to see the poem as a moral, spiritual allegory of redemption and salvation through suffering, purification, and spiritual enlightenment. In recent years a trend towards mystical interpretation has also developed, interpretation which sees some sort of complex, esoteric symbolism running through the whole poem. In the early years of the century, however, the established school, especially in America, was that of the realists, who insisted that the literal meaning of Dante's works referred to real events, not fictive, and that the works were thus autobiographical in tendency. (In other words, Beatrice was a real woman, Dante was really in love with her, etc., etc.) The symbolist school arose in opposition, and its premises were best expressed by J. B. Fletcher (Dante, 1916; *The Symbolism of the Divine Comedy*, 1921). According to Fletcher, all reality was symbolic to Dante, and the higher allegory was merely the inner truth of reality. It follows, Fletcher argued, that the reality or fictiveness of events recorded by Dante is immaterial, just as it is immaterial whether Dante subsequently read back symbolic meaning into poems already written; the end-product is what matters, and there poetry is merged with the symbol in the poet's mind.

Regardless of the specific approach, however - and this is true even of the extremes of esoteric symbolic interpretation - what underlies the bulk of modern Dante criticism is the will to see the *Divine Comedy* as an organic, integrated whole. As G. A. Borgese has put it so aptly in his essay "On Dante Criticism" (1936), "the history of Dante criticism is, broadly speaking, the process of recovery or discovery of structure and unity from scattered gems of beauty amidst barbaric obscurities"; and as more of these gems were recovered to the sensibility, a more complex view of the poem emerged. But the old problem that agitated the minds of eighteenth-century critics reasserted itself in modern guise with Croce's attack (*The Poetry of Dante*, 1922). The Italian philosopher of esthetics condemned the *Divine Comedy* as having no poetical value as a whole; he just granted it some lyric and descriptive passages of beauty. Basing himself on Edgar Allan Poe's dictum that a "long poem" was a contradiction of terms, Croce carried pre-Romantic and Romantic criticism to its extreme by totally dissociating the structure of the poem from what constituted, strictly speaking, poetic beauty. Hence, according to him, the *Divine Comedy* was nothing more than a theological romance spiced, as it were, by occasional passages of lyric poetry. Admirers of Dante naturally came to the defense of their poet; as late as 1960 Irma Brandeis, in the preface to her *Ladder of Vision*, refers to Croce's attack and presents her study as undertaking to reveal the integrated nature of *the Divine Comedy* by showing that Dante's meanings throughout are fused in his images. Much earlier Santayana (*Three Philosophical Poets*, 1910) and T. S. Eliot (Dante, 1929) had insisted on the wholeness of the poem. And the scholarly-historical school, too, has come to approach Dante's poem as an organic, integrated structure. Thus Joseph Mazzeo, introducing his *Medieval Cultural Tradition in Dante's Comedy* (1960), announces its intention of exploring "some of the most important principles of structure of *the Divine Comedy* and their relation to characteristic ways of organizing experience in medieval intellectual culture."

The story of Dante criticism is thus the story of a steadily accumulating body of notions and insights as well as specific facts, now, in the twentieth century, organized into an integrated view of the *Divine Comedy* as a richly endowed and highly articulated organic whole.

THE DIVINE COMEDY BY DANTE

. . . .

Question: In what sense is *the Divine Comedy* an epic?

Answer: *The Divine Comedy* may be termed an **epic** because, a long narrative poem depicting the experience of a central hero, it seeks to present a universally true picture of life. The fact that the hero's experience is imaginary does not make the truth it discloses any less real or universal. For in his journey through Hell, Purgatory, and Paradise, Dante looks at human actions and their ultimate consequences; he learns to judge human experience in the light of the eternal principles by which the life of the universe is regulated. *The Divine Comedy* deals with human destiny, and seeks to understand it.

What is at issue in Dante's poem is not the outcome of a national war, but the salvation of a soul. In a Christian world, this is the most important issue of all - in the last analysis it is the only issue that really matters. But souls first come to life in this world. It is in this world that they encounter the many forms of evil, and it is in this world that they must make the choices which will affect their ultimate destiny and destination: An evil choice may land them in Hell for all eternity, while the operation of a moral conscience may yet save them for Purgatory and Paradise. Consequently, *the Divine Comedy* must of necessity concern itself with the world in which the temptations of evil exist and in which determining choices are made. The poem thus seeks to uncover the universal meaning behind the multitude of human events that make up life.

Finally, since the hero's experience is spiritual, it is valid for all men. Dante's situation is common rather than unusual - like most men everywhere, he has been caught in the tangles of practical, everyday living, and has lost his way. He despairs of salvation, and his situation would be hopeless if not for the grace of God, which sets him back on the true road by taking him through the realms of the afterlife. There he learns the nature of evil; there, too, he purges himself and disciplines his moral will; and there he is shown the full meaning of the spiritual principles which underlie not only human life, but the life of the universe. By the time he has reached the end of his journey, he has absorbed the lesson with the vision, and is ready to return to earth and reveal what he has seen. In so doing, he enlightens the rest of mankind by showing the true nature of human existence.

Question: Why is Dante the hero of the poem?

Answer: Dante makes himself the hero of *the Divine Comedy* because only by being strictly faithful to his personal experience - i.e., his vision - can he communicate the truths that have been revealed to him. If we are to understand and feel his experience, we must identify with him; and if the process of identification is to take place, he must stage himself as the hero. What happens to him then happens to us, and this experience of ours holds out the promise implicit in Dante's experience: that God is equally interested in the salvation of each of us. Besides, by making himself personally involved with what he sees, Dante involves us with it, and once we become involved, we begin to feel that his pilgrimage is not just an academic exercise in ethics and theology, but a meaningful experience. Dante's moments of fright, his fainting spells, his joy - all these are reminders of the fact that his is a human, not a supernatural experience; and if it is human, then it has as much relevance for us as it has for him.

Question: What is the nature of Dante's experience in Hell, Purgatory, and Paradise?

Answer: In Hell Dante is presented with insight into the nature of evil. Evil, he discovers, cannot be explained; it is something which has to be seen. But it is not something set apart from life, either. It is woven into the pattern of day-to-day living, and as Dante descends from circle to circle, a real panorama of human life passes before his eyes. Before he can undertake his own spiritual regeneration, he must drink in the total vision of evil (hence Virgil makes him look squarely at Lucifer). And what he sees is appalling in its monstrous stupidity. For that is what is at once so horrible and so sad about evil: It is terribly stupid because it is self-destructive. Invariably, it springs from the misdirected human will-either lack of proper control over appetite, or perversion of the will brings it into being. Yet whether Dante pities (in the case of Paolo and Francesca) or condemns (Fra Alberigo), the consequences are invariably the same: The sinners are cut off from God, the source of all light and joy. In Hell, Dante takes a long, hard look at mankind and its ways; only then, having faced the horror and the disgust, is he ready to move towards moral perfection.

If Dante's journey through Hell provides him with an uncompromisingly realistic appraisal of the life of the world, his journey through Purgatory is designed to bring him to a point of moral perfection from which he can rise to the understanding of divine mystery. It is educative in a **didactic** sense, and *Purgatorio* teaches by preaching at Dante. The symbolic purgation of the seven deadly sins leads him to the earthly paradise, where the true order for human existence is revealed to him in the symbolic pageant of Church and State. Dante's experience in Purgatory stands as a corrective to what he has encountered in Hell, but the correction is intended not only for Dante but for the whole world: The proper regulation of life on earth will eliminate much of the evil encountered in Hell - guided by the divinely sanctioned institutions of Church and Empire, mankind may hope to regain a measure of the perfection it lost at the time of the Fall.

In Paradise Dante's experience is purely spiritual. This does not mean that there is anything vague or woolly about it; it simply means that what he encounters is the reality of spiritual truth. It is there that he learns the great principle that regulates the life of the universe: Peace consists in harmonizing one's will with that of God. The freedom of the individual will is therefore defined, and then God's justice. All that Dante experiences is designed to strengthen him for that moment when he will look directly upon the Divine Presence, but essentially, throughout *Paradiso* there is a dual path leading to God, one complementing the other. For spiritual reality must be known as well as felt, and Dante's mystic surge is kept under the control of intellect. (Dante even insists, with St. Thomas Aquinas, that knowledge comes first since love is born of knowledge.) The final mystery is, of course, unfathomable. Dante is given a glimpse, but he can barely recall it; nonetheless, that vision is the vindication of all he has undergone on his way to the summit, and it promises redemption, not only to him, but to all who would do like him.

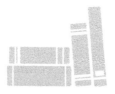

BIBLIOGRAPHY

Auerbach, Erich, *Dante, Poet of the Secular World*, Chicago: University of Chicago Press, 1961.

Barbi, Michele, *Life of Dante*, translated and edited by Paul Ruggiers, Berkeley - L.A.: Univ. of California, Press, 1954.

Bergin, Thomas G., *Dante*, Boston: Houghton Mifflin, 1965.

Brandeis, Irma, *The Ladder of Vision: A Study of Dante's Comedy*, London: Chatto and Windus, 1960.

Cosmo, Umberto, *A Handbook to Dante Studies*, Oxford: Basil Blackwell, 1950.

Croce, Benedetto, *The Poetry of Dante*, New York: Henry Holt and Co., 1922.

De Sanctis, Francesco, *De Sanctis on Dante*, Madison: University of Wisconsin Press, 1957.

DeSua, William J., *Dante into English*, Chapel Hill: University of North Carolina Press, 1964.

Eliot, T. S., *Dante*, London: Faber and Faber, 1929.

Ferguson, Francis, *Dante's Drama of the Mind*, Princeton: Princeton University Press, 1953.

Friederich, Werner P., *Dante's Fame Abroad, 1350–1850*, Chapel Hill: University of North Carolina Press, 1950.

Gardner, E. G., *Dante*, London: Oxford University Press, 1921.

_____, *Dante and the Mystics*, New York: Dutton, 1913.

Gilbert, Allan, *Dante and His Comedy*, New York: New York University Press, 1963.

Grandgent, C. H., *Dante*, New York: Duffield, 1916.

Mazzeo, Joseph Anthony, *Medieval Cultural Tradition in Dante's Comedy*, Ithaca: Cornell University Press, 1960.

Santayana, George, *Three Philosophical Poets*, Cambridge: Harvard University Press, 1910.

Sayers, Dorothy L., *Introductory Papers on Dante*, London: Methuen, 1954.

Stambler, Bernard, *Dante's Other World: The Purgatorio as a Guide to the Divine Comedy*, N.Y.: N.Y. Univ. Press, 1957.

Valency, Maurice, *In Praise of Love*, N.Y.: Macmillan, 1958.

Vittorini, Domenico, *The Age of Dante*, Syracuse: Syracuse University Press, 1957.

Vossler, Karl, *Mediaeval Culture: An Introduction to Dante and His Times*, 2 vols., New York: Harcourt, Brace, 1929.

Wicksteed, P. H., *From Vita Nuova to Paradiso*, New York: Longman's, Green, 1922.

Williams, Charles, *The Figure of Beatrice*, New York: Noonday Press, 1961.

Lightning Source UK Ltd.
Milton Keynes UK
UKHW020716290922
409643UK00009B/905